Come One, Come All!

Come One, Come All!

DRAWN
FROM
MEMORY
BY

Don Freeman

RINEHART & COMPANY, INC.
NEW YORK · TORONTO

Acknowledgment is made to the following publications, in whose pages some of the theater drawings and lithographs first appeared: *The New York Times,* the New York *Herald Tribune,* the newspaper *PM, Theater Magazine* and *Stage.*

TO

Roy

I would like to thank all my friends for their patience along the way, with particular gratitude to William McCleery and May Falk for their early words of encouragement.

PART ONE

PART TWO

PART ONE

PART ONE

1

A SHORT TRIP

*T*HE NOTION of coming to the big city must have sprouted when I was a mere weed of six or seven and altogether too young to do anything immediate or practical about it. I like believing that I know exactly how this notion took root and how it grew into full bloom in spite of various stubborn and yet natural obstacles.

My story begins when the world was a town named Chula Vista, a place especially designed for kids to stub their toes on. Here in Chula Vista, California, a few miles above the border of Mexico, I remember discovering that I was alive and free—to a certain extent.

Life in those days seemed to consist solely of freckles, pepper trees, and a woman named Mrs. Blass. More than anything else her presence became the inevitable obstacle standing in the way of complete freedom. Through certain arrangements which were not made entirely clear to me at the time, Mrs. Blass had become the guardian over my brother Warren, myself, and a boy named Botsford Beverforden. She was extremely strict and appropriately plump, endowments which would have been perfectly acceptable to us had she not also possessed a zealous urge to remake the rest of the world in her own image and likeness.

Botsford's parents were both living at the time; however, they were living apart from each other. His father, I remember hearing, was in the consular service attached to some country as distant as

3

Siam, while his mother shivered in Alaska. Mrs. Blass had come into the picture opportunely by contracting to care for Botsford until his far-flung family could pull itself together.

My brother Warren, having four more years to his credit than both Bots and myself, was allowed a comparatively free rein while we two were held in firm check. Any failure on our part to toe the line brought forth cool beads of perspiration on Mrs. Blass's brow like the early morning dew on a pumpkin—a condition we gradually learned to recognize as the first sign of an impending storm.

The mesas of Mexico were clearly visible from our house and the three of us were under the illusion that Pancho Villa the notorious bandit might be running wild about that territory. My daily aim was to capture him and bring him in alive to Mrs. Blass, who could mete out justice like nobody else. But no matter how severe her punishments, the one thing she never tolerated was tears, and when they appeared they had absolutely no effect on her. In this respect she bore a remarkable resemblance to the unique plateaus that rose stolidly along the horizon. These abrupt land formations had stood their ground throughout countless centuries of rainfall, and they now re-

4

mained as impressive warnings for us three squirts not to try eroding the stern crust of our taskmistress by pouring forth mere feeble tears of resentment. A stronger solvent had to be found.

Yes, the mesas and Mrs. Blass were the very spittin' images of each other. I began diligently observing her character from close range with the serious intent of determining just what was her weakest point, and when this was found I would set to work dissolving her stubborn will. The only hitch in this procedure occurred when I realized that all along she was also busily making a study of *my* weakest points under her penetrating microscope. No wonder, then, that we kids often felt akin to small plants and branches that were constantly being grafted and cultivated; we too were pestered and pruned, all the while trying to grow naturally under hothouse conditions.

But unfortunately for Mrs. Blass, she had picked on three rather tough twigs. The private tussle threatened to loom into the battle of the century, and indeed would have had she not suddenly one day eased her grip and decided to take me along with her on a two-day trip to the city of Los Angeles, much to my bewilderment and delight. I hurriedly gathered my crayolas and drawing paper, intending to make a record of our adventures into the outer world. Warren and Bots were stunned that she selected me to accompany her on this brief pleasure trip; as for me, my whole outlook on life did a somersault! I felt I had misjudged her; under her rock-ribbed façade must beat a kind heart after all! Hadn't she always given the impression that she loved Douglas Fairbanks and her pet canary Gretchen more than all three of us boys put together?

Nevertheless, once en route to Los Angeles every semblance of discipline vanished. My crayons could hardly keep pace with the sights outside the train windows. No color seemed bright enough to catch the brilliance of the green groves of orange trees stretching endlessly past the rugged purple mountains on one side and the intense blue Pacific on the other. I leaped over everyone's lap in an attempt to capture the passing scenery and also found that the passengers were irresistible subjects for drawings—especially the man who snored all the way.

From under a vast straw hat a beaming smile broke across Mrs. Blass's usually ferocious countenance, indicating that she was even

more excited than I. In all likelihood she had cooked up this excursion as an excuse to cut loose from her ruthless routine, taking me along solely to salve her conscience. During the train trip an amazing and heretofore unsuspected side of her character emerged, a knack of whipping up lively conversation with every gentleman within casual radius, a performance that made me wonder how she could be the same woman who fed chickens and kept us kids on the jump. The world outside Chula Vista presented inexhaustible material, and by the time we reached the Los Angeles station the sketchbook had been filled. Mrs. Blass, thinking she had found a perfect solution for keeping me out of mischief, immediately bought several more drawing pads.

The city seemed to have changed her—she treated me as though she were half saint. For lunch, for instance, we went to a shop called the Pig'n Whistle, where she ordered not just one but two malted milk shakes both of which she said were mine. For herself she ordered what I have since learned was a fudge parfait. But this was only the beginning. The next indulgence on our dizzy whirl was a movie. We saw one of those deep-sea mysteries in which two divers fought it out in the eerie depths of a gluey sea, attacking each other over a sunken treasure chest while they were being assaulted by starved man-eating sharks and menacing octopuses.

It may have been an excellent picture but it didn't set well with my two malted milks. Before the finish of the film I wobbled into the open, under escort, just in the nick of time.

It seemed good to be safe on dry land again and we walked along a few blocks soaking up the beneficent sunshine. But Mrs. Blass was not for wasting much time sauntering—suddenly she grabbed me gently by the arm and insisted we find a Fairbanks picture. She said she also needed to get rid of the deep-sea feeling.

We hunted everywhere for one of his movies but none could be found. I caught myself feeling sorry for her. But she didn't give up easily. Undaunted, she burst forth with the bright idea that her Doug might be in the actual process of making a motion picture. The movie studios were only a few miles away from the center of the city by street-car, and in those days anyone with the mildest interest in moviemaking could walk unmolested into the studios; he might even be welcomed as an extra in mob scenes.

As we arrived at the studio a snow scene was being filmed. I can still see the piles of salt heaped on all sides while the California sun blazed down. The energetic director and cameraman wore their caps

8

backwards. The scene looked very strange from where we watched—an old hunter lost in the wilds of the frozen North surrounded by mountains made completely of salt. After each shot the actor had to take off his heavy fur coat, sit down under a palm tree, and mop away the perspiration.

Taking advantage of my good behavior, Mrs. Blass left me and wandered off looking for her favorite screen hero. Not long afterward I found myself caught up in a mob scene. All the stray extras and visitors who could be enticed were called into action for the filming of a city sequence. For me this experience was about the best thing that could have happened. I had lost Mrs. Blass and for the first time I became part of a crowd.

An hour or so later when Mrs. Blass came back, disappointed by her fruitless search, she found me stuffing my pockets with discarded rolls of exposed film, and it was here she decided to call it a day.

By sundown we returned to our downtown hotel opposite a beautiful, tall-palmed park. After a big dinner I undressed and jumped between the neat, cool sheets, whereupon Mrs. Blass tucked me in and, while her good-night kiss was still moist on my cheek, disappeared into the night. Just where she went and what she did I never knew or ever dared ask, but I strongly suspected that she found a Fairbanks picture. Certainly I must have needed to plunge headlong into sleep but my eyes would not stay closed; the experiences of the long day ran through my mind over and over.

9

As I lay restlessly in bed, the clanging of the streetcar bells in the busy street below made about the most wonderful sound I had ever heard. I got up and went to the window and for a long time watched the people walking in the park and on the sidewalks. Before I finally fell asleep that night a conviction formed in my mind: small-town life was not for me! Right then and there I decided to get me someday to a city—the sooner the better and the bigger the better.

2

THE RITUAL

ONCE BACK in Chula Vista it became obvious that the trip had spoiled me for sure. The country and I had absolutely nothing in common, excepting of course the proposition of putting up with Mrs. Blass.

On the surface this excursion appeared to have no great effect on my guardian, for she adroitly changed back to her same old baffling self. Only gradually did I begin to suspect that the trip might have affected her as it had me—a yen for adventure began smoldering deep inside her and there was no hiding it. This yearning began manifesting itself in the strangest ways imaginable. We thought something was peculiar the first time she started reading tea leaves, but when it grew into an after-supper ritual, we knew her mind was wandering on a magic carpet. Then, too, there were the nightly consultations with a Ouija board which she had bought in Los Angeles and secretly stashed away in her suitcase.

She soon found meanings in everything from spots on the moon to spots on her new living-room rug, omens in flowers, clouds, and even assorted religions; but the Ouija became the most dependable medium of all. She claimed that this device foretold such events as travels to the Orient and who was to be my future bride. Forever delving into my matrimonial future, she would try to find out where I was going to settle down and bring my wife, because wherever this was to be, she intended being there, making toast for our breakfast. It was all beyond me, but I went along with her fancy figments. Anything to keep the perspiration from blooming on her brow!

Hardly a day or a cloud went by but that Mrs. Blass attempted to seek out some momentous symbol. Her attitude toward cloud reading assumed almost portentous proportions when, regularly at the day's end, she took to holding consultations on the back porch. With hands on hips she breathed in deeply and lifted her head heavenward and communed. The soft fleecy clouds as they gyrated in the vermilion sunset said things to her that none of us could possibly grasp.

I remember watching her through the back screen door one warm Saturday evening during one of these rhapsodical ceremonies. In her usual stance, and breathing more deeply than usual, she was searching the heavens for omens. Even from inside the kitchen I could hear her powerful breathing. I didn't think she knew I was snooping but she had a very accurate sixth sense.

Taking a stab in the dark and without turning around, she called out sweetly, "Donnie Boy? [an expression that irked the daylights out of me every time she used it] Donnie Boy, come outside and stop sneaking up from behind me like a tarantula! I want you to behold something out here with me."

I obeyed promptly. She took me by the arm and lifted my chin so that I stared straight into the blinding sunset. "Now tell me," she said, "what are the clouds saying? Can you read anything in them? The signs are ever so clear to me tonight. Mountains. Oh, such beautiful, gorgeous high mountains! They probably mean we will be traveling together one of these days, far away seeing the world. They must be the Alps—yes, the Swiss Alps!"

All that I could make out of those voluminous puffy forms were piles of whipped cream with perhaps some strawberry sauce poured over them. I was hungry. Mountains I just couldn't see.

"Wouldn't you love to go climb to the peaks of those magnificent ranges one of these days?" she went on rapturously. "They exist especially for us to enjoy, you know. Tonight it comes very clearly to

11

me that you and I will one day be standing on the snow-capped heights of St. Moritz." Then she added, "What do you see, dear?"

"They look to me more like the hills around Descanso," I said. The mere mention of this ghost town, in the sticks about thirty miles inland from where we lived, pricked her balloon, and Mrs. Blass gave my arm a yank—I knew retreat was advisable. Straining at the sky again but still without seeing mountains, I told her that I could maybe make out great colored swirls like the silk turbans the Turks wear.

"Well, now, isn't that interesting!" she said. "Yes, yes, I can see them too. They probably mean India and Constantinople and such places. Well, aren't we traveling tonight! Now let's inhale three times and make a wish."

We did, and the ceremony was over.

3

AN OMEN AND A FLOOD

WITHOUT a doubt the brightest and most anticipated event of the week came on Sunday—the day my father traveled out to see us. It was his only chance to shower us with affection, as he worked hard the full week in a clothing store in San Diego eleven miles away. I believe he lived for this day just as much as we lived for the few hours we could be with him.

Each Sunday he would bring us presents—always three of a kind; although Botsford was not his boy, he was included in everything. Sometimes he brought clothes, sometimes games, but always he remembered to bring me drawing materials.

My father also never failed to carry along his square box camera to record our Sundays together. Being a man of few words he expressed his delight in life through these photographs. I can see the square camera now, covered with dark-brown leather all worn at the corners. When we went on a hike to the hills, he recorded every phase of the journey as if it were a travelogue into the interior of darkest Africa.

We longed for the day when we could live in San Diego and see my father more often. Happily, sooner than we dared hope, this move was unexpectedly precipitated.

It all began the day Mrs. Blass suddenly fell victim to an urge to make soldiers out of us. None of us knew what had come over her. She started out by lining up the three of us in the middle of the hot, dusty road and ordering us to right face and left face. A few of the other kids in the vicinity saw us and ran to join our ranks.

Mrs. Blass then fitted us all out with sticks for guns and this equipment attracted still more recruits. She shouted several commands at the top of her lungs, and lemons dropped from nearby trees. Soon she had us marching up and down the long road. As I recall, everybody got a kick out of this sudden call to arms. Everybody but me. I worried about it. What had got into her? Where was the war? Who was our enemy? I was always the one wanting to know the whys and wherefores of such matters and consequently she had some difficulty keeping me in line.

The sun still had a full half day's beating down to do and the road was already hot enough to bake potatoes. Mrs. Blass strutted ahead,

13

marching her barefoot army for a mile or two back and forth, halting us at frequent intervals and having us do about-faces until it ceased to be a joke.

While we were still a good way down the road it became necessary for me to fall out of line and sit down under a tree. This broke the morale and brought forth from General Blass a torrent of rage such as a top sergeant should have envied. She dismissed her platoon and ordered me to march back to the house. This I did, but I had to limp all the way on my heels. Large blisters had formed on the soles of my feet.

Mrs. Blass went to the kitchen through the front door and waited there for me to hobble in. I thought by her expression that she planned to make me part of the chili con carne that was cooking on the stove. But on examining my feet she soon discovered that I did have good reason to fall out. Switching her character in a second, she became a Florence Nightingale. I was told to get in bed while she rushed to put a basin of water on the stove.

Later that evening as I sat on the edge of the bed eating con carne (a dish, incidentally, which she was a past master at making), Botsford and my brother Warren came in and watched me soaking my feet in the hot-water basin. For them this was fascinating business. Botsford held his ears, waiting for the blisters to pop, but nothing happened beyond a sudden clap of thunder outside.

As it began to rain the evening cooled—but my feet didn't. A good long hour of downpour went by. While my brother dried the dishes, I sat soaking—still nothing happened. The evening proved to be very uneventful for the expectant audience.

As for me, I wasn't any too anxious to be rid of the blisters. They might come in handy as an excuse for not having to drill the next day. It appeared quite obvious that Mrs. Blass had plans for an extensive course in military preparedness. She had already heard rumors of the approaching World War and she must have envisaged herself winning it singlehanded. Taking the blisters to bed with me that night, I listened to the rain falling determinedly on the roof and against the window-panes. Never before had it come down with such powerful impact. Mrs. Blass rushed around to see that all the windows were shut tight, since the water had already begun coming in through the cracks.

14

Violent rolling thunder and flashes of lightning finally put me to sleep appropriately dreaming of Noah's Ark.

The following day we learned that floodwaters were rising rapidly only a few miles away. Everyone in the neighborhood was in a panic.

When Mrs. Blass came running into the house screaming, "Quick, boys, pack everything! It's a flood! Do you hear me? A flood!" I jumped from the bed and that did the trick—there were no more blisters.

While the trunks were being packed Mrs. Blass remembered she had to phone a moving van to come and collect us.

"Is this the Heck Brothers movers?" she shouted over the phone. "The people who moved me from San Diego two years ago? Well, I want you to come right out here and rescue us from the floodwaters! Yes, I said 'flood.' If you don't come we'll be swept out to sea! Now get a move on, you! I have three boys and we're all packed and waiting for you!"

Her generalship of the day before helped frighten the Heck Brothers into action, for they agreed to come right over. I believe we were the only people in Chula Vista who felt the danger seriously enough to make such a drastic move. Within two hours and through three inches of rainfall the movers splashed their way to our front porch.

I remember seeing the huge truck with the large red-lettered slogan on the side: BE MOVED BY HECK! The men were ready to haul us away—chickens and all. Curiously enough, Mrs. Blass seemed almost pleased as she rustled around packing up, but we knew why: only a short time before, she had been talking about having her heart set on our sometime going to live in San Diego, where she owned a small house. This flood obviously had come as an omen from above. She was a great one for finding omens in everything. Noah never had a more direct message from the Almighty than did Mrs. Blass when she called the Heck Brothers.

Three husky movers carried the furniture out of the house in double time with our guardian shouting directions and demanding that each piece be handled with great care. Last to be put in the van were we three kids—stuck in the back end as a last-minute appendage where the rain ruthlessly showered in on us. Mrs. Blass, holding the bird cage containing Gretchen, the canary, on her lap, sat in the front seat with the movers. Gretchen suddenly took to singing after having been sullen for several months.

The van finally pulled out and all but floated down the road. The sky was still dark and the unmerciful rain seemed to show no signs of ever stopping. We were on our way and mighty glad of it. From the loose canvas backflap in the rear of the truck, we could see the terrible havoc caused by the downpour.

As the van drove along the edge of the lowlands, we caught sight of a piano floating by and on its top, which barely stuck above the surface, stood a drenched hen weathering the storm in solitude. This was to be our last view of Chula Vista.

4

SAN DIEGO

SAN DIEGO in those days purred along like a contented cat. Not that the inhabitants were in the least bit lazy; they just seemed to surge ahead but in one place—and a more beautiful place for such placid movement could not possibly be found. From nearly every window in the entire town the view of the bay was almost inescapable. However, our house on Kalmia Street had many windows but none of them exposed the bay, which was perfectly all right because we had other things—kids next door. I wanted neighbors more than I wanted a view. I had had all the scenic wonders I needed. The floodwaters would hold me for a long time.

I daresay that Kalmia Street held more life and energy than any other thoroughfare in town, most of which to be sure was expended by one family in particular, the Bartletts. Mrs. Bartlett had several children, with another always in process. Some of their names are implanted in my memory like a sailor's tattoo: the girls' names were Delight, Joanna and Rosemary and my special pals were Squeek and Legler.

The houses themselves were two- or three-story affairs, ours being by far the funniest: a two-story square stuccoed contraption with a windowed topknot called the solarium. In this solarium Mrs. Blass kept all her precious keepsakes, such as a pair of crutches that once belonged to her deceased husband, several charcoal portraits of relatives and one of a very small boy in a lace collar, wearing long black stockings (we were never told who he was). Also hidden among her souvenirs was an old violin which is to play a part in this narrative presently.

17

It got to be a full house, especially when my father came and lived with us. He had the room next to mine and it did begin to feel more like home. Although we rarely saw him during the week, since he rose early and worked late, just knowing he was close by helped a lot. Ever so faintly I could recall having felt this sensation of home before. That was during the brief period when my father and mother and Warren and myself lived together on A Street, farther downtown. Of my mother I remember only her frailty and strong devotion.

Having my father in the same house—well, it was like having somebody on your side, though he never interfered in any way with our appointed guardian's sense of direction. Mrs. Blass had been recommended by a close friend of my mother's, and in her last long illness she had asked her to help care for us. Though circumstances prevented my father from being with us as often as he would have liked, his move to Kalmia Street was a reminder of a dim and pleasanter past and it brightened up the somewhat disjointed present.

The greatest adjustment for living in the town of San Diego came with learning to wear shoes. After this quaint custom was accepted, there was nothing else to do but live abundantly within the limits of Mrs. Blass's eagle eye.

My brother Warren, four years older than myself, continued giving evidence of being the complete master of his own destiny. I stood in awe not only of his capacity to make the most of his freedom but of the style in which he accomplished the trick. Like Gaul, Warren was divided into three parts: part bird, part fish, and the rest high-powered enterpriser. His favorite sport was climbing to the topmost diving platform and throwing himself headlong into space, eventually landing with a neat splash in the bay below. His flights on a self-built motorcycle became the terror of the town, and it was somewhat difficult to understand then just how the speed demon in him combined with his more practical and somber side, that of engaging in projects which in their modest way always seemed to pay off.

The manufacturing of ice cream by means of a washing machine was among his greatest achievements at that time. Together with a pal of his he churned out a variety of strange and original flavors. Their scheme of mixing fruit with milk and then freezing it put us younger squirts in the shade with our lemonade stands. Of course I had reason to suspect that the washing machine had something to do with the originality of his products. Once in his search for a new taste sensation, his exploitations led him to the idea of concocting a sweet-potato ice cream which, needless to say, came out as a financial fizzle though it did make him famous for miles around. As far as I know, no one had ever made sweet-potato ice cream or, for that matter, had ever cared to.

For some reason Mrs. Blass never gave the slightest evidence of recognizing the fact that Botsford and I might also be getting older. In spite of this oversight, we managed to build quite an eventful and adult world within the boundaries of our back yard. We started making movies. Out of three crutches and a cigar box and two coffee cans we created a motion-picture camera. After school Squeek and Legler and sometimes Delight would join our company and the rest of the day would be spent rehearsing western serials at breakneck speed and with fiery imagination.

I had an irresistible urge to be director for these thrillers and inspire the neighborhood actors to put everything into their daring leaps off the roof of our barn; and I made the most of my safe job by putting my cap on backwards and crouching dramatically while turning the crank, which was originally part of a coffee grinder.

Mrs. Blass also expanded her activities. She accepted a job in a nearby public school teaching a class of thirty or more pupils geography, mathematics, and matrimony. I was perhaps the happiest kid on the block when I heard this—anything to keep the weight of her attention from falling entirely on me. But as luck would have it—or as she probably went out of her way to arrange it—I was placed in all of her classes. This meant the spotlight had to be constantly on me as she tried to make me her prize pupil. After a month or so she found my unfailing ineptitude much too embarrassing and soon thereafter I was assigned to three other teachers, Miss Sharp, Miss Peil, and Miss Haberman. It was good having other women in my life for a change.

Our living in San Diego really gave me the hoped-for chance to see my father more often. Saturday afternoons were usually spent with him in the clothing store where he worked for a gruff boss named Mr. McCusick. For a while Mr. McCusick had me convinced that he was a bear in human disguise, as he succeeded in scaring me whenever I arrived at the store asking for my father.

"Your papa eese not here any more!" he would sometimes growl, or, "I fired your papa yesterday. I don't know where he eese now!"

But always a few seconds later I could see my father far back in the long store selling overalls. Under that fearsome mustache, I began to suspect, Mr. McCusick hid a grin two miles wide. While my father and another salesman were busy taking care of the colorful customers, I loved going around sniffing the store; the clean smell of the new suits and overalls was something special. The overalls made you want to get to work.

As the mornings progressed Mr. McCusick would generously allow me to sit in his office and make drawings on the back of invoices and bills. From there it was possible to look out through the glass windows and see the customers. The store had in stock only inexpensive union-made clothes and they were sold to working people who were for the most part Mexican and Chinese.

When I wasn't busy sketching the customers I wandered around the block inspecting the penny arcades and ten-cent movies that showed hair-raising serials, the story content of which I stored up for our own back-yard after-school productions. Saturday nights I had the privilege of eating dinner with my father, and whenever he didn't work in the evening he would take me to see the local stock company's stage shows. These were rare and memorable moments for me. My father loved the theater and rarely missed a production if he could help it. Together we saw such plays as *Checkers* and *Seven Keys to Baldpate*. We would sit in the balcony and take turns looking through a small pair of opera glasses which he greatly prized.

Everything about those evenings at the theater was ardently relished: sitting next to my father waiting for the show to begin, the music from the orchestra pit, the hurried scanning of the programs, the silken rustle of ladies settling in their seats, even the gaudy asbestos drop curtain advertising the various local merchants' wares, all added to the drama of the event. But the most exciting moment was always sure to come when the asbestos curtain lifted swiftly to reveal the rich wine-red velvet curtain onto which played the warm glow of the foot-lights. The house lights dimmed and then silence—the cue for the show to start! On stage another world of full color, singing, and rapid talk. However preposterous the plot of the play, it now hardly mattered for the spell had already been cast. I believed whatever the actors cared to have me believe. With crafty persuasion they immersed their audience in the numerous petty complications of the lives of people whom we had not even known existed. This sort of convincing artifice seeped into my system through every gullible pore and made me lastingly susceptible to the theater's magic.

Someday I would have to find out all about how they made it work.

No matter how impressive these high-class performances were, I believe the ten-cent movies of the wild westerns and Chinese opium dens stuck most vividly in my mind. Also the movie machines in penny arcades opened my eyes wider to the strange and forbidden life from which Mrs. Blass had tried her best to shield me. The weekdays following reflected these excursions. Scenes in Chinese opium dens suddenly became the subject matter for several days' shooting in the back yard. When Mrs. Blass found all the neighborhood innocents painted up and smoking long pipes, however, this trend in our scenario subjects came to an abrupt end.

About this time Mrs. Blass seriously began to worry about my future. Hardly a day went by without her trying to induce me to take up one of the higher arts. In the evenings after study hour she played

Galli-Curci records while Botsford and I sat in the front room squirming in our seats. We had a hunch this long-haired music was a form of torture since we observed that she always found some reason for being in the kitchen during the concerts.

Without ever directly opposing her plans, my father had a way of throwing in a subtle sort of lifesaver. As a present once, he gave us the famous laughing record called "The Cornet Solo" during which a concert cornetist suddenly breaks down in the middle of a solo and laughs throughout the rest of the record while the audience joins in with contagious guffaws. Whenever possible we would put this record on in place of Galli-Curci as a relief. Our doing so inevitably brought Mrs. Blass from the kitchen distressed and more doubtful than ever of someday making me into an operatic singer.

She also tried the piano on me, but that didn't work either. I paid attention to the clock instead of the metronome. Then one day she found an old violin which had once belonged to her sister Grace, back in Cassopolis, Michigan. Immediately she insisted that finding this

22

instrument was a positive omen that I should become a violinist. She tried it under my chin, just for size, and unfortunately it fit. I even *looked* like a violinist to her! She began to have elaborate visions of my becoming a virtuoso and going on tour throughout the world, beginning at Carnegie Hall. To be sure, I had always anticipated seeing the world, but I didn't care for the idea of holding a violin while doing it.

All this was but part of a well-knit strategy to pump out of me every drop of latent talent, come hell or high C. She had a long-range plan—make no mistake about that. She had me buffaloed for I never knew what whim would seize her next. At other times, however, she had me feeling I could love her if only she would just take it easy and not rush me.

I became suspicious about ever being a violinist when after the tenth lesson my auditory nerves started buckling, convincing me that I had no business fooling around with the sacred instrument—besides

I had too much respect for the neighbors, and for Botsford in particular. Soon thereafter hostilities broke out between myself and the violin teacher, hostilities which tended to overshadow the fact that World War I had already begun.

Soon the war spirit penetrated all our activities. Fighting became the main subject. Even our back-yard movies dealt with nothing but war horrors and combat. Often these make-believe battles turned into vicious realities when tin cans filled with ashes were hurled like hand grenades back and forth between the rival gangs. I broke up the battles when I took to wearing my father's old, baggy Spanish-American War uniform, the spectacle of which effectively frightened off my opponents. Everybody became hysterical with laughter, doubled up with glee, and went home.

Since I showed little talent for the so-called art of warfare, I conveniently began staying indoors every afternoon after school and clipped and copied the political cartoons of the day. A set of the Book of Knowledge also kept me very well occupied when I wasn't outside winning wars. My father had given them to me and had built a rack right alongside my bed to hold them.

I devoured their contents avidly and liked best reading about a certain city built on an island named Manhattan where all kinds of people from all over the world had come to live. To prove it they showed one page after another of photographs of fabulous sights. I was half convinced by these pictures and also slightly suspicious that they might all be fictitious. Someday I would just have to pack up and go there and see for myself. Those pages etched even more deeply my longing for a great city, and now that city had taken concrete form—it was New York.

5

THE FLIVVER

*A*FTER THE WAR Mrs. Blass was one of the first to ride the wave of the future. She considered herself a pioneer, so it was no wonder that she became one of the first women in that part of the country to buy and drive a Ford.

Before she bought it, the salesman nearly went crazy trying to teach her how to drive. She hated to admit that anyone could show her anything but after ramming the car into a stubborn telephone pole one afternoon she was forced to change her attitude. This little experience taught her that a machine does not run on personal magnetism alone.

The salesman would gladly have given up the deal after two days, but doubted he could ever resell the car since Mrs. Blass had made it into something peculiarly her own. He must have breathed a deep sigh of relief when she handed him a check and finally dismissed him. After this transaction, hours were filled with talk about her new Ford sedan. She spoke of it in terms as tender as those she used in speaking of Douglas Fairbanks.

About this time she hired a helper, a very sweet and gentle country girl named Hortense, who fortunately had neither the ability nor the inclination to talk back. Hortense and the Ford inherited the same characteristic—they had endless endurance.

The entire household now anticipated with dread the day when Mrs. Blass would insist on our driving to the country for a Sunday picnic, a treat she had held over our heads for two full weeks.

Shadows of coming events cast themselves across the kitchen table early one Sunday morning in the form of deviled eggs. I was the first to foresee the terrible thing about to come and I quickly tried inventing a case of measles, but as the fatal hour neared, Mrs. Blass caught me daubing my face with red paint. I was instructed to take the water-color box and several sheets of paper and pile into the back seat of the Ford, which for the past several days had been poised obediently inside the garage.

After much running back and forth loading the car with supplies adequate for an expedition to the North Pole, we all managed to squeeze inside. Hortense sat silent in the front seat next to Mrs. Blass, who made quite a process of putting on her new driving gloves. They were large and bulky and she undoubtedly believed they were indispensable. Botsford and I sat in the back seat not saying a word, inwardly shuddering. Lucky Warren was off swimming in the bay that day and my father had gracefully begged off, although Mrs. Blass had hoped he would join us.

After a few minutes of silent prayer Mrs. Blass began looking around for the ignition switch. We held our breath. She found it. Then, turning the switch to one side, she became flustered because nothing happened. She fretted for a second, trying to figure out what to do next. Botsford, who had a slight mechanical aptitude (he slept with a hammer and a pair of pliers under his pillow every night), suggested that she try putting her foot on the starter. Botsford soon wished that he had no aptitude at all.

Turning around, her face aflame, Mrs. Blass said, "Young man, I'll thank you to let me handle this machine myself! I need no instruction from anyone! Another word out of you and you can just stay home . . . we can very easily leave without you, Mr. Beverforden!"

Botsford knew there wasn't a chance of her sticking to her word so he didn't take her up on the generous offer.

Once again our guardian adjusted herself in the front seat, spreading her arms like a pelican about to take flight, and sitting up so straight that her bosom all but covered the steering wheel. Botsford and I clutched our seats and Hortense made herself as small as possible, keeping a safe distance from the driver's undulating elbows. Finally her foot contacted the starter. The car began backing out—she had evidently guessed the right shift for reverse.

"Keep an eye out the back window for me, dearie," she called in a saccharine-soaked voice. "Tell me if the coast is clear."

26

I assured her nothing was in sight for five miles: the coast was clear and the alleyway was all hers! Then I closed my eyes.

The latch to the garage door somehow caught hold of a rear fender and the door itself was left dangling on its one loose hinge as we moved jerkily down the alley. The neighbors came running to their back gates, staring at us as if we were off in a rocket to the moon.

My mind goes blank when I try to reconstruct the trip and just how we ever made it far out into the country that day. All I know is that we did make it. Our senses must have been so numbed by the perilous adventure that nothing registered except the fact that Mrs. Blass drove us not only nearly to distraction but to an old schoolhouse she had heard about some fifteen miles away near the town of La Mesa.

This schoolhouse, surrounded by drooping palms and pepper trees and tired ropes from the playground swings, provided what Mrs. Blass contended was a perfect place for a picnic.

Owing to the strain of the trip and the fact that Botsford had taken Mrs. Blass's scolding, *not another word out of you!* literally, he stayed mute as a mummy, and after we had all disembarked it became apparent that something special was afoot for me. Mrs. Blass casually reached back into the sedan, which was still panting from its ordeal, and pulled out the box of water colors. As she handed it to me she said in her sweet Sunday falsetto, "Now, dearie, you just go ahead and paint to your heart's delight. That's why we came all the way out here today. There is so much beauty on all sides for you to paint, you just go off and create something somewhere!"

28

Naturally I had no more urge to create anything from these depressing surroundings than I had to sing like Galli-Curci. Not that there wasn't *something* to make a picture out of here; the site had plenty of possibilities—what soured me was the idea of being told what to paint. I don't suppose she knew that this experience settled forever and instantly my future course. I could never be anything but a free-lance artist.

During the picnic's stagnant hours I mulled over an idea for a drawing of Mrs. Blass as she looked driving the flivver. This picture became so deeply engraved on my mind that nothing else mattered. That evening, after a miraculous return trip, I locked myself in my room and feverishly made a crayon drawing of her from memory, which I suppose was my first effort at creating a cartoon. Once this had been put down on paper and was satisfactorily out of my system, I felt that the day had not been a total loss. But before turning out the light I tore the drawing into a hundred small bits and carefully deposited them in the wastebasket—just in case.

6

LOVE NET

ROUNDING out my guardian's character without alluding to her romantic tendencies would be like asking Rubens to paint the Three Graces with their clothes on. Love was a topic no one in our household managed to steer clear of for very long. As might be expected, this condition was generated by the Queen Bee herself and I had the opportunity of learning firsthand something about the life of the humble bee while we watched our house grow into a hive honeycombed with intrigue. Her wards were but drones and slaves in her fervid designs.

Although not yet in our teens, Botsford and I found ourselves in the same fix as Hortense, who was at least of marriageable age: the three of us were caught in Mrs. Blass's waxworks. Warren escaped her matrimonial machinations since no one could ever tell him who should be his sweetheart. He had a girl on every block and not even Mrs. Blass could control him. But, as I say, the rest of us were good and stuck. Of us three, Hortense, who was about as aggressive as a butterfly, seemed the one least likely to succeed in ever planning a love life of her own—that is, if the notion ever crossed her mind.

Unhappily, this was the girl for whom Mrs. Blass had already picked a mate.

As a first matchmaking enterprise, she successfully kindled a sure-fire romance in which the only difficulty was keeping the flame alive. The young man in this triangle lived at the time in Cassopolis, Michigan, making it necessary for Mrs. Blass, as well as the distance, to lend whatever enchantment there might have been. We knew only two things for certain: the young man worked as a bank teller and his name was Sylvester. All other details of how he happened to get messed up in this frame-up were clouded in a mist of family complications.

After the customary exchange of photographs, a series of letters started filling our mailbox. The mailman in Michigan must have been busy too, probably carrying the greater part of the burden, since Mrs. Blass lightly dashed off a steady stream of love notes with the agility of a bird warbling its wooing song. Hortense never chirped a word of her own. Not in my wildest imagination could I ever see her penning Sylvester a mash note.

The day was not long in creeping up when the inevitable letter arrived from Cassopolis stating the bank teller's proposal of marriage. I could hear the clanking of handcuffs slipping around poor Hortense's wrists while Mrs. Blass read aloud to us his promise to come to San Diego as soon as it was practically possible. Hortense all but wilted into a cipher before our eyes.

This was indeed a sad scene, but Hortense's pitiable plight moved me only to the degree that it portended the dastardly coup awaiting me. Yes, at that very moment a honeyed cell was being craftily built up around *me,* of all disinterested drones! All I wanted was to be left alone and to make movies. Love was for the birds. Had I happened

30

to entertain any such ideas, they would certainly have favored Alicia, the Mexican girl who lived across the canyon.

Having reached the ripe age of nine, I became involved in the most unconscionable plot ever cooked up this side of the Garden of Eden. Mrs. Blass put aside for me a girl by the name of Ada Staley who lived on a lemon ranch in Escondido and played the cello. Whenever it worked out, Mr. Staley would bring Ada along the day he delivered our monthly crate of lemons, and sometimes Mrs. Blass would invite her to stay overnight in the solarium. In truth, Ada was all right. There was actually nothing the matter with her, she had everything any cello teacher might want in a pupil—but I was no cello teacher. Nevertheless, the two of us were wantonly being woven into a heavily brocaded plot which took us years to untangle.

How can I ever forget the night Mrs. Blass first announced that she had seen the girl of my dreams in her tea leaves? We had just finished an especially grueling dinner and Mrs. Blass was sitting opposite me sipping the last drops from her third cup of hot tea while I tried downing a dish of parsnips. The taste of those parsnips still lingers in my mouth.

Obedient Botsford, as always, found himself in the difficult straddling position of trying to stay in Mrs. Blass's good graces and at the same time remain a pal of mine. On this night I sat admiring his act of juggling a tray of stacked dinner dishes while kicking the kitchen door open with his foot. But more than this I admired his ability to eat parsnips without wincing. Hortense ate them, but she winced. Warren? Well, he hardly ever ate with us any more, as he was forever camping out in the hills with his Scout troop.

The tenseness of the situation can best be explained by saying that William S. Hart was playing at the Cabrillo Theater that night and, unless I choked down the dish waiting before me, none of us could see the movie. This accounts for the daggered stares Bots had thrown me during his dessert. But for Bill Hart I would do just about anything so, pinching my nose and closing my eyes, I valiantly did away with the entire portion of parsnips and waited for compliments from the hostess. My gallant performance went unnoticed, however, as Mrs. Blass was deep in her tea-leaf reading.

Overhead the light from the stained-glass chandelier flooded the

31

tabletop. A bread crumb shone out on the highly polished mahogany in lonely relief. Tiny moths fluttered around the lamp batting themselves crazily against the hot light bulbs. The clock on the mantel in the next room ticked out the name of Bill Hart. Bots and Hortense continued with their kitchen duties. Dried-up blossoms from the fuchsia plant that hung over the portico gently floated to the floor.

From across the table I could see plainly the tea specks left sprinkled around inside Mrs. Blass's cup. Someone had to break the silence, so I said, "Ain't that a heart shape in there, Mrs. Blass?"

She persisted in her study with one hand resting under her chin exactly like the picture of "The Thinker" that hung on the wall behind her. She raised the cup toward the light in order to get a more distinct view of the contents and then began moving it in a circular motion while she twisted her head around.

I grew dizzy watching her do this. Suddenly she snapped her head back into its socket and asked, "What was that you said just now, dearie?"

Startled at her attention, I repeated my observation. She pulled her chair close to mine and handed me the cup. It seems I had spotted the perfect symbol; she would be putty in my hands from here on—but I didn't want to go too far with this thing; I wanted to go to the movies to see Bill Hart.

"Well, I do declare!" she said, palpitating. "You are absolutely right. Here it is, a perfect heart shape."

The tiny, brownish-green particles looked completely formless to me but, foolishly sinking into my own mire, I asked what did she suppose they meant?

"Well, it can't mean two things," she said. "It can only mean one thing—someone's in love! And the problem is now to find a sign which will show us just who this could be!"

In what resembled nothing so much as a lot of seaweed swept up on a white beach, Mrs. Blass saw scattered music notes which indicated that Ada Staley's name was sure enough being dragged out out of the sediments. I tried playing dumb.

"Why, look her, dearie, just look where the lemon rind is placed. You know I always believe that the rind has a great deal to do with the reading. Here it is like a bridge joining the heart and the music

32

notes. And do you know what I think it is trying to tell us?" She continued without waiting for my reaction: "It can't mean anything else but Ada Staley who lives in Escondido on a lemon farm and you. You're both musicians, you know."

"Good night!" I said, pushing my chair away from the table.

"What was that you said, young man?" she asked angrily.

"I only meant that Ada ain't in love with me! She's always talking about the other boys all the time."

"Never say 'ain't,'" Mrs. Blass scolded. "How many times must I tell you not to use that expression? There is no such word, not in this house nor in the English language. Besides, I happen to know from Ada's father that she is very fond of you. And why not? It is perfectly logical—you are a violinist and she is an accomplished cellist. You *should* both like each other!"

Clearly the time to thrash out this whole subject was then and there. Bill Hart could go jump in the bay.

"Yes, but, Mrs. Blass," I protested, "liking a girl is different from loving a girl, isn't it?"

She thought a moment before speaking. "Well, either you believe in these signs or you don't, and when you've been around as long as I have you'll begin to know something about such matters. Just you wait, things will turn out pretty much the way the signs point."

Here she realized that she had probably gone beyond my depth and her approach changed to one of chumminess. "Darling, you know I don't want to force anything on you," she said almost apologetically. "I'm only trying to smooth the path. I want you to find the perfect girl, so I am going to be very particular, that's all. Wouldn't you love to have a fruit farm in Escondido to come back to after traveling around playing concerts? You and Ada might very well play duets together, you know. Of course you would have to find someone to accompany you on the piano."

Mrs. Blass mused on until it came time for us to go to the movies. I didn't dare interrupt her glowing mood. No doubt about it: she was what you call just plumb tea-happy.

7

THE OUIJA BOARD

*I*T WAS LIKE my father to know exactly what I wanted without my ever having to hint. For my tenth Christmas he gave me a present of a shiny brass trumpet. Bots was no happier with his Indian bicycle than I with the brand-new horn when I discovered it under the tree, sparkling in an open leather case lined with brilliant green velvet.

However much my father respected the classics, he was unable to go along with Mrs. Blass's vision of seeing me sawing away on a violin or singing in an opera. He modestly admitted preferring the popular dance music of the day to the heavier stuff, and nearly every week he brought us the latest recordings of the Dixieland Jazz Band. The blues was just being born about this time and we wore the grooves off W. C. Handy's "St. Louis Blues" before the record was three days old.

No directions went along with the gift of the trumpet because my father knew the problem of learning how to play the instrument would have to be my own worry. But there was no worry to it. Whenever Mrs. Blass went out of the house I turned on the records and sat next to the Victrola and blew myself red in the face. Eventually I got wind of how to play scales and a few other essentials, and after several months I played along with the best recorded orchestras in the nation.

Mrs. Blass probably felt about my playing the horn the way I felt about her weakness for the Ouija board. But blowing a horn seemed to me to be harmless, while having to play Ouija every night with her was not merely boring, it got to be downright alarming.

After clearing away the dinner dishes she always went straight to the cabinet and brought out her Ouija set. We could never quite tell

34

whether she was serious about this game or not. As a matter of fact, she would not have called it a game. Perhaps it was only a part of her search for the truth, which went along with a peculiar propensity for finding omens in everything. If she had to have an omen and have it fast, the Ouija board always obliged.

One momentous night directly after dinner, Mrs. Blass seemed especially desirous of getting an answer on some important matter. The tone of her voice as she ordered Botsford and me to sit down at the table and open up the set should have been sufficient warning to us that this was to be no ordinary session.

"Place your hands on the board!" she said vehemently, settling back in her big chair. "We are going to ask a very important question of Ouija tonight and I want you both to concentrate!"

We snickered. Mrs. Blass seemed to be in good spirits and we took it for granted that she must be kidding.

"All hands on!" she called, with her eyes closed. "I will ask a

question and we must have absolute quiet! This is the question: is someone at our table going away on a long trip?"

All six hands rested on the small flat block that is supposed to move slowly around the board and stop in front of words such as Yes and No and the various letters of the alphabet, thus spelling out the answer; but as it happened the small block failed even to budge.

Mrs. Blass opened here eyes and said sternly, "Someone is not concentrating, *someone* is holding us back!"

I looked at Bots, who was certainly concentrating as hard as I was on *not* letting the block move, just for the fun of it. This was a Friday night and in all likelihood Mrs. Blass would take us to a movie. She knew the one way to make the block move; she said, "Maybe, if we get our answer, we can all go to see my Doug! You both know he's playing tonight in *The Mark of Zorro* at the Plaza."

The block began to slide almost imperceptibly around the board. We knew that some mysterious force was getting her the answer she wanted and it was going to move the block to the word "Yes," which is exactly what occurred. We thought now that she had her big question of the week settled we could run upstairs, put on our coats and get going to the movie. But no! Mrs. Blass had another question to ask.

"Now, dear Ouija," she went on, "since we know that one of us is going away on a long journey, I want to ask which one of us will it be?"

We concentrated. I have no idea what possessed me at that time, but I recall wanting very much to be the one who would go away on a trip, preferably to New York, and little did she suspect how I felt. She also had that strong yen for adventure. It was a case of my yen against hers, clearly, and I could easily have let her win on the Ouija board that night, but instead I decided to concentrate on the letters of my name. There was a tense moment when the block tried to spell out Carrie, which was Mrs. Blass's first name, but instead it moved to the letter D and stayed there. Nothing could move it. At this moment Bots and I looked up and noticed the wet, hot beads broiling on her forehead. But the warning sign came too late.

She glared at me as if I had done something against the mystic gods of Ouija. "Young man, you can march right upstairs to your room and go straight to bed!"

36

I couldn't even say, "Who, me?" I was that dumfounded.

Little chance of stalling around when an order came from her in that mood! By the time I was in bed I heard their excited preparations before taking off. Hortense was loudly enticed into going along in my place. The front door slammed and I was alone in the house with only agony and anger for company, cursing myself for having given in to the bright idea of making the Ouija spell out *my* name. That evening seemed interminable. The movie must have run longer than *The Four Horsemen of the Apocalypse*, but trying to imagine what new daredevil tricks Douglas Fairbanks might be up to in the picture made it just that much longer.

Hours later, when they finally came home, I pretended to be asleep, but I could hear only too clearly their ecstatic chatter about what a wonderful movie it had been. Just to make matters worse they had not seen *The Mark of Zorro*—they had seen Charlie Chaplin in *Shoulder Arms* instead!

The following morning I continued to smolder inside and with the still hot embers of scorn a plan began to brew. After making quite certain that Mrs. Blass had gone out of the house and the coast was clear, I rolled up a few clothes in a small bundle and ran downstairs, through the back door, out through the back gate, and down the long alley. My feet carried me faster than I had ever thought possible. It seemed that I was being drawn by some magnetic force. I didn't look into any of the back yards, fearing *she* might be visiting a neighbor, and with my eyes and chin facing front and cutting the wind, I ran to the end of the long alley and then slowed down to a trot.

Unwittingly I turned the corner and started hurrying again with my heart pounding furiously, when suddenly I realized I hadn't the slightest idea where I was going. In my desperation plans had never been formulated further than the end of the alley. It was useless to run to my father, situated as he was, working day and night. Wasn't he doing all he could for me? As for running across town to my grandmother and Aunt Julia, my mother's family, that was out. I knew they would have no alternative other than to return me promptly into Mrs. Blass's legal, caressing clutches.

Finding myself blocks away now, I stopped and leaned against the side of a barn. There in the shade I caught my breath and gathered up my thumping senses. A few moments of the deepest soul-searching ensued. I thought of my mother. What would she have had me do? Certainly she would not have wanted me to run away in the first place. An imaginary argument took place. Reluctantly I tried to forgive my guardian; after all, she was doing her best to keep me from growing into a burglar or an automobile salesman; she had my interests at heart. Without being able wholly to admit or understand it, I knew I really felt sorry for her. There came a sudden impulse to turn back. Slowly and sheepishly I began backtracking up the long alley where only a few minutes before I had been breaking all speed records. I could at least be glad that no one, as far as I knew, had witnessed either the frantic escape or the frustrated retreat. Hortense was the only one who possibly might have seen me. As I came through the kitchen, it was obvious that she sensed I had been up to something. I ran to my room, fell on the bed, and bawled.

The emptiness of the house that warm Saturday afternoon was

38

intensified by the raucous noises of my companions playing outdoors. Inside something unaccountably strange permeated the house, a feeling that this was no ordinary day but a day of decision.

By the time Mrs. Blass returned home my eyes were dry and I sat alongside the Victrola in the living room blowing away on my horn as if nothing had happened. Crude dissonances filled the room as I fooled myself into believing I was playing in Paul Whiteman's orchestra. These discords no doubt prevented me from hearing the chugging of the Ford sedan as Mrs. Blass guided it into the garage, bumping the sides as gently as a ferryboat forcing its way into a slip.

I was so startled to find her standing there in the doorway of the living room that I dropped the horn from my lips as if I had been doing something wrong and gave a wrinkled half-smile. For a second I didn't quite know how I *should* feel. The Victrola continued to spin the record of "My Wonderful One."

Mrs. Blass broke the tension. With more than a trace of solemnity in her words, she said, "I want to see you when you finish practicing. I will be in my room upstairs."

A cold ripple went down my back. She had never before admitted that playing along with the records constituted practicing.

"Yes, ma'am," I answered.

Proceeding to put the trumpet in its case, I nervously waited for the record to end the last chorus. Then I placed the record in the rack and went upstairs. Mrs. Blass's door was shut, so I knocked.

"Come in," she called in a gentle voice.

Without having yet taken off her large white straw hat she was sitting in a rocker near the front window. Directly in front of her was another chair in which she indicated I should sit.

"Come, sit down. I want to talk to you," she said.

There had been only one other occasion of such a serious nature; that was the time she had informed me of my mother's death. Mrs. Blass was in much the same frame of mind now, except that on that former day she had held me on her lap.

The events of the day had been such that I came already adjusted to hear the worst. She began by holding my hands and looking me straight in the eye and saying, "Do you recall our little experience at the Ouija board last night?"

39

I swallowed. I should have known I hadn't heard the last of that. "Yes, ma'am, I do."

"Well, I want you to know—" she halted a moment as tears began and then went on—"I want you to know that it was correct."

"What was correct, Mrs. Blass?"

"Why, the Ouija board! It said you were going away. Don't you remember?"

From a cage over in the corner of the room, Gretchen gave forth a lusty chirp aptly filling in my void.

"Yes, you are leaving me. It was decided this afternoon at a meeting with your father and grandmother. You are to go away to boarding school. I promised your mother that when you were ready I would relinquish my responsibility. You see, your grandfather—your mother's father—willed you a modest sum and left it with the stipulation that you attend a boarding school of your mother's own selection. *He* was strong for boarding schools; of course I have other opinions. However, I shall carry out your mother's wish. I'll confess I've dreaded this day. I never wanted you to leave me. But your father and the rest of us thought it all over and they think the time has come."

As she was saying these last few words, she had my head pressed tightly against her and her arms locked around me, almost smothering me in a sudden burst of affection. By the time Hortense came to the door to tell us dinner was on the table, we must have been completely wrung dry.

8

UNCLE ED AND THE REDWOODS

*M*RS. BLASS'S influence steadily and naturally dissolved once I had gone away to school, and yet new obstacles such as an academic education and several strenuous summer intervals continued blocking the way to freedom, an idea which to my young mind had become synonymous with the notion of getting to New York.

It is one thing to dream and another thing to dare, and what I needed most then was the daring. Frankly the thought of going away to the big city had me mightily frightened and as the time for the inevitable take-off grew imminent, the more monstrous grew my fear. And still no one was forcing me—only myself.

So far no one had ever believed that I was really serious about this. Whenever the subject came up I noticed that my classmates waxed terrified at the thought. They were puzzled; how could a half-cocked high school cartoonist have ideas of surviving in the gargantuan metropolis? For two summers I had earned a scant living by blowing a horn in dance bands, but doing anything practical with artistic efforts had me scared stiff. And then I figured, well, maybe they had something there—just how *did* I think of managing the venture?

Far beneath my surface bravado I shook at the prospect of having to earn that first nickel from my pencil.

Only one thing remained unshaken, the desire to go.

But it would be good to have someone else understand and perhaps egg me on a bit.

The redwoods of northern California hardly seem a likely locale for finding the kind of encouragement I needed, yet this was where my busy Uncle Ed, who ran an auto camp, gave me a helping handshake.

His being at heart an expert photographer might have had a lot to do with his knowing so much about the deeply gnawing problems of a would-be artist. This happened the summer I was long, lanky, and seventeen. I had accepted the job of working in the camp primarily so that I could be near my father, who was helping his brother for the season. The clothing store in San Diego had folded. Besides seeing my father, I probably thought that working among the world's tallest trees might be a good conditioner toward living someday among the world's tallest buildings.

As I stepped off the hot and dusty bus in front of the general store in the redwoods that warm July day, I was confronted by a large welcoming party. After having been away to boarding school for so long, it would have given me pleasure enough just to have seen my father there alone, but beside him stood a flock of relatives headed by Uncle Ed, all giving out with a lavish greeting.

I'll never forget Uncle Ed—how he looked dressed up like a woodsman but without an ax, wearing leather puttees, a green and red plaid shirt, and a warped state trooper's hat. As he slapped me on the back he shouted, "Jumping Jehoshaphat, boy! How you've grown! You were only a little runt when I saw you last. Now look at you, almost as tall as one of my sequoias!"

Then he caught sight of my trumpet case. "Good boy, you've brought along your horn and, say, can we use you in our orchestra! We've got a dandy dance pavilion and there's dancing nearly every night!"

And then suddenly the greeting party broke up and everyone went back to work.

From that moment things started going so fast that I saw very little of the sky or found scarcely any time to be conscious of the breath-taking beauty of the magnificent trees surrounding us. I didn't even get to see my father very much. For every member of the family there was plenty of backbreaking work—one chore after another, dishes to be washed, cabins to be cleaned, sodas to be jerked, and gas to be pumped.

No tourist ever drove into this auto camp without at once becoming aware of Uncle Ed's explosive presence. Not that he was the braggadocio type, he just assumed the responsibility of seeing to it

42

that each and every visitor who drove into the grove was given the proper scientific introduction to "his" trees. It was as if he had planted them there himself, that's how close he felt to the towering monarchs.

He could be very certain that few of his guests had ever met up with such specimens in their travels. Even before the tourists had time to dust off their clothes or unpack their luggage, Uncle Ed would have them gasping and straining their necks scanning the heights of the trees.

"You're looking at the largest and the oldest trees extant," he would say proudly, while twisting a cigar from one corner of his mouth to the other, a cigar which he never had time to light. "We have here most magnificent specimens of the *Sequoia gigantia* whose ages range between five hundred and thirteen hundred years! It's said that these big trees were first discovered around here in the year 1852 by a hunter in pursuit of a bear. This particular *gigantia*," he would conclude, as he patted the bark of the tree beside him, "is 280 feet high with a diameter of thirty-six and a half feet."

It was as if he were trying to sell something. He never used the ordinary tourist term "redwoods" when he spoke of these trees. It was always *Sequoia gigantia* and the words rolled from his lips like those of a radio announcer describing some tasty new sauce.

There in all the startling outdoors and freedom Uncle Ed managed to be the most involved man in America, running ninety miles an hour all twenty-four hours. Not only was he going full speed, but he had the rest of us doing likewise. I was very fond of Uncle Ed although I never could get five minutes alone with him. I wanted us sometime to have an art-to-art talk. One day toward the end of the season the chance finally came.

The general store in the auto camp offered everything any tourist might want, including money. The cash register sat in plain sight on a counter in the middle of the store and frequently there would be no one in the store to wait on the customers. Sometimes when I came in to mix a drink to quench my own thirst I found my father the only member of the family trying to handle all these clamoring customers. People milled around the stock and some even mixed their own refreshments behind the counter. Of course, I would come to my father's rescue during these predicaments by helping to serve the customers and, incidentally, trying to save the cash register.

But these rescue missions were misunderstood. Uncle Ed seemed to have implicit trust in human nature except in the case of his relatives. On this particular occasion he rushed into the store and found me surrounded at the fountain.

He started yelling, "Say, boy, why aren't you over at the gas station? People are trying to get gas! Can't you hear them honking? What in the devil are you doing here?"

There wasn't a chance to answer him.

"What in the Sam Hill are you doing, drinking sodas again? Eating up all the profits?"

I tried to explain that the soda fountain was all out of charged water but he wouldn't listen.

"Be right with you, folks!" he said to the crowd as he tied an apron around his waist and waved me aside.

I was almost out through the back door when he called to me, "Hey, boy, I can't make sodas without charged water!"

Being Big Chief Water Charger around there, I knew only too well what this meant.

"Folks," he hollered, "don't go away. We'll be serving sodas in just a jiffy!"

"But what about the gas station?" I asked, knowing full well he had forgotten about the honking horns.

"Just get back there and start rocking the tank, boy! One thing at a time!"

This meant going to the supply room at the rear of the store, where the process of charging water involved my sitting on top of a small tank which rested on two wooden rockers and rocking back and forth, an exercise recommended for reducing which I hardly needed at the time. An air-pressure tube was attached to the tank, and this pressured air into the water, thereby charging it.

The supply room was cram-jammed with all kinds of commodities, large bottles containing syrups of every flavor and color, boxes of candy, and cigarette cartons by the hundreds. Also stuck away in this small room were rolls and rolls of photographs of the redwoods which Uncle Ed had taken. Magnificent photographs!

45

When we lived back in San Diego, my father had often told us that his brother Ed once took pioneering trips into the redwoods, traveling by means of a broken-down wagon which made its hazardous way through the unexplored forests long before any high-powered highways had been built. He usually had gone on these trips with hunters who brought back bears while Uncle Ed shot and brought back beautiful photographs.

These were the very photographs that I now unrolled as I rocked back and forth on the water charger. It was hard to believe that they had been taken by the same man who was at this moment in the front of the store dishing out chocolate-marshmallow sundaes. The more I rocked the more I became convinced that he was a great photographer and should return to the camera. Slipping off the tank, I began to look around the room to see if his camera might be hidden away.

Just as I discovered part of his old equipment beneath a large cooky tin, Uncle Ed opened the door. He was furious. He wanted to know what I was doing off the rocker. Then he wanted to know what I was doing with his old camera.

"And what are all my photographs doing unrolled?" he shouted as he belligerently leaped onto the tank himself and began riding it like a broncho buster in a wild West show.

"Listen, Uncle Ed," I said, knowing I had to make my point then or never, "they're wonderful photographs! Why don't you take some more sometime?"

He was shocked, but he rocked on.

"Can't you see I haven't got time right now? You know how busy we are. Jumping Jehoshaphat, son, you see me running around here every day. When in Heaven's name do I get a chance to take pictures?"

His voice softened, for he knew I admired his prints, and he said, "You really like these photos, don't you?"

Now we were both looking at them. "I'll tell you a secret," he confessed, chewing on his dead cigar. "I kind of like them myself. Yep. I have to get the darn things out once in a while and look them over. Did you find the prints I made at the San Francisco Fair? They're in here someplace. I was official photographer for the whole blame shebang!"

He had been off the rocker only a few minutes but before he realized it and got sore I eased over and climbed on to finish the job.

"Yep," he said, and he wasn't yelling this time, "let's get that water charged and out into the front fountain. We'll make a go of this camp yet, and then I'll go back to my camera work."

He lit his cigar, forgetting the crowd for the first time. "You know, you ought to take up painting," he said. "I saw that picture you painted on the big slab back of the kitchen there. Take my advice, boy, go to New York and follow it up."

I almost fell off the tank.

"You really mean it? You think I should?"

"Why, certainly. Wisht I'd a done it when I was your age. New York's the only place to go if you want to get the best schooling, and that's the thing you oughta do, study. Don't fool around with that there horn. Maybe you can use it to earn your way, blowing in some orchestra, but soon as you can you oughta take up art serious. Don't let anybody trick you out of it. I say if anybody's got a hankering to go there that's what they oughta do. There's them that don't have a hankering and that's a good thing too. So I says to you—go!"

"Thanks, Uncle Ed," I said. "I will."

"Well, let's get rocking! This is the biggest Saturday we've had yet and, besides, the governor is stopping over with us tonight!"

He winked at me as he went out the door.

By the end of the summer I knew I was paid in full by this little talk of ours, and what was even more, I had been fully convinced that Uncle Ed knew what he was doing—he needed no advice or encouragement from anyone, least of all from me, for his life's work was the enjoyment of living and at that he was a master.

9

GRADUATION GIFT

*A*FTER RECEIVING that spiritual kick in the pants from Uncle Ed, I went back to school where I had only one more year to serve before graduating. My attributes as a student can best be passed over, saving untold embarrassment all around. It is enough to say that I did graduate, though hardly with honors. It is a pleasure to recall that commencement day, since I know I will never have to relive it.

As the solemn exercises began, terror seized me. From out of nowhere a telegram appeared. It was handed down the long row of frigid classmates and I knew it was addressed to me. I imagined its contents: STEP OUT OF LINE CALCULATIONS SHOW DISCREPANCY IN GRADE MARKING MAKING IT IMPOSSIBLE FOR YOU TO GRADUATE.

But I was wrong! The telegram contained an invitation from my grandmother to come to San Diego and take a summer course in art—her graduation gift to me!

It had been an unquestioned intention to make for New York immediately, but my grandmother's gift offering disarmed me and the enticement was irresistible.

Studying art in the San Diego School of Fine Arts, situated in the midst of beautiful Balboa Park, had its value, although at first staying in San Diego seemed like a retrogressive step and it bothered my conscience. But soon I found that drawing from the nude model and studying anatomy were important activities and I became increasingly grateful to my grandmother for her present. There was one slight hitch to all this, however. In the evenings at the dinner table when I expressed amazement and delight over discovering how beautiful were the female form and the intricate construction of the human body, my grandmother became quite alarmed.

And yet, as the weeks went on, it was impossible for me to conceal my astonishment when my drawings from the nude began to look like human beings, especially when I squinted one eye. Instead of being pleased to hear how well I was beginning to grasp the human form, my grandmother grew seriously concerned over what she called my "attitude." She claimed I showed very little humility and was much too conceited over initial results.

"You *must* learn to be more humble," she said sternly one night while we were at dinner.

Actually I hadn't the vaguest idea how to go about getting that way.

"If you don't know, it's time you learned," she said. "And you will certainly have to step down off your pedestal of self-esteem before you can go to New York even if it takes another year."

It took quite a little while for the significance of her statement to soak in, but when it did I began eating humble pie in earnest. The graduation present had strings attached which let me know that I was not so free as I thought—not yet.

The director of the art school was an artist of unusual ability, and seriousness. As he came around to each student's work, he would make drawings of the nude figure with telling finesse on the corners

49

of our papers. Next to his, our graphic attempts appeared crude, but all in all it was probably a helpful thing to see what a really good drawing looked like.

During the model's rest period one morning I felt like making a series of cartoons of the various members of the life class and used the edge of my drawing paper for the purpose. When the director came around to criticize he was furious at my frivolity. Apparently he didn't believe anyone should enjoy life in a life class.

After this incident he regarded me with distrust. Throughout the following rest periods I hardly moved while waiting patiently for the model to resume her pose. I indulged only in the harmless pastime of looking out the classroom door where I could observe the new students as they came in to sign up at the registrar's desk.

While thus absorbed one morning I saw the sight of my life. A girl dressed in a white coat stood waiting her turn at the registrar's desk. Simply standing there, she made the most beautiful work of art I had ever seen. Something about her simplicity together with the brightness of her look made me say to myself, "That's the girl for me!"

From the time she entered the life class it was impossible for me to keep my attention on the model. I noticed that the new student had already half finished her first figure drawing while I sat fumbling with my charcoal and erasing meaningless scribbles. I was lost in admiration.

It was useless to try to draw. I decided to concentrate on anatomy. I had a small book demonstrating the workings of man's muscular system which I propped up in front of a large drawing board and made a serious effort to study.

In the middle of the afternoon the director entered the room to make his daily rounds and from a distance mistook my anatomy book for something of a trivial nature. He hastily concluded that I had gone hopelessly to pot.

In a loud and cutting voice he announced, "Young man! Yes, you there reading the magazine, you with the dreamy look—gather up your materials and leave this art school at once!"

True, I was in a thick mist but his words pierced it like a foghorn. I held up the anatomy book in a feeble attempt to explain, but his mind was frozen.

"I've had all the nonsense I can stand from you," he continued. "We have no room for bench warmers in this life class. You are dismissed!"

Outside the building I hung around waiting for the class to end in order to speak with the new girl. A sympathetic look from her as I left (or what might have been interpreted as one) made me hope that she might walk through the park with me if I invited her. She accepted and we walked across the Cabrillo Bridge and talked together. Even though she didn't have all the facts in the case, she was most sympathetic. When I said how much I wanted to see her again she was not averse to our going sketching together some Sunday. I didn't take her all the way home that afternoon but I did put her on the streetcar.

Dizzy with the events of the day, I then faced the problem of telling my grandmother the awful news of my getting kicked out of her graduation present. With all the humility I could muster short of crawling, I approached the front door. There was a note placed over the bell informing me that my grandmother had suddenly fallen ill. I went quietly up to my back room and waited for Aunt Julia to explain what had happened. When she came, she told me it wasn't

51

anything terribly serious, but my grandmother needed rest and quiet and perhaps, for the time being, it would be best if I found a room elsewhere. I agreed. After Aunt Julia had convinced me that I wasn't the cause of grandmother's sick spell, I felt all right and I didn't mind one bit looking for a place of my own. Actually a suitcase was never so excitedly packed. Not a word was mentioned about what had occurred at art school that day.

I found a room on the other side of town, on Hermosa Street, and spent several mornings in the public library, where the sanctity of these walls became a refuge for reflection. I read Dickens, Dana, and Robert Henri's *Art Spirit*, and looked through all the popular magazines studying the illustrations. But all this was evading the issue. I knew I could no longer put off the idea of having to start earning a living. Art and illustration and the cool library were all right, indulgences certainly to be desired, and yet they were luxuries that had temporarily to take a back seat.

The trumpet my father had given me for a Christmas present many years before still came in handy, and once in a while I found myself torn between a life playing the horn and a life using the pencil. Whenever I heard Bix Beiderbecke play cornet solos on the latest recordings I would have put my soul in hock to have been able to blow hot licks like his.

In my room on Hermosa Street I kept a small secondhand portable Victrola, and if I hadn't been able to hear a few records every day, life then would have been an empty salt shaker. The elderly landlady must have been totally deaf. I can't believe she too was a jazz fiend! She never complained even if I played a record over fifty times trying to catch the pure Bix licks. In those days this musician Bix was recognized as the solid saint of jazz; later he became a god. His music melted steel; his horn was a torch blazing the Blues and ripping the heart apart. Any trumpet player with half an ear considered him a master, and I was no exception. One day I even forgot to eat on account of him. A new recording called "Singin' the Blues" had just been released and it had Bix at his blistering best. I played along with his elusive solo hour after hour, so long, in fact, that my lips started bleeding. But I got the solo set in my mind, I felt I "had it." Anyway I was now ready

52

to go out and get a job in some dance band, any band that would give me the chance to sit in and show how I could sound off. I joined the union and the daytimes thereafter were spent hanging around the music stores in town.

One music store in particular became the hangout for the local dance band musicians. The boys meandered in, talked shop, and listened to the latest recordings. The manager didn't seem to mind our using his store for a meeting place; he didn't even seem to mind the fact that we hardly ever bought records. Perhaps he was smart and wanted the store to *look* busy. It was a pleasure to assist him in this way and one stack of records after another went the rounds in the record booths. I thought the height of bliss would be to marry the daughter of the owner of a music store and settle down in a record booth.

Orchestra jobs were picked up either inside the store or outside under the awning, depending on which place was the cooler. To pay my New York train fare plenty of musical notes had to be blown from my trumpet, and eventually I had no trouble securing small-time engagements for nearly every night.

I played my first job in a tough boxing arena on the sailor side of San Diego, in a five-piece band. Our job was to strike up tunes immediately after a fighter hit the canvas for a K.O. The leader of the band knew more about boxing than he knew about music. He could tell to the punch how long the boxers would last, and before they went down for the count we had our instruments poised ready to rip into a chorus of "If You Knew Susie Like I Know Susie."

Another time I joined a bunch of hot musicians who persuaded me to play down in Tia Juana with them. It was against the law for anyone under twenty to enter Mexico for work but I needed the job, so I tried to look legal when our car was inspected at the border.

I liked these boys in the band and we made fairly warm music together.

The block-long saloon where we played filled up so fast that no one paid any attention to our music. The noisy crowds guzzled at the bar and the dance floor sagged with a mass of heavy feet. Every fifteen minutes "Drinks on the House" was announced by a blaring fanfare on my trumpet and a long roll of the drums.

About midnight one night a wild husky Mexican woman took a notion to climb on the music platform and muss up the musicians' hair.

Clumsily she knocked over the music racks and as she came toward me, I ducked.

"You're no twentee-year-ol'," she slobbered as she tried to muss my already haywire hair. "Who smuggled you across the border, eh, keed?"

Suddenly the influence of the western serials welled up in me and I shoved her off the music platform with a mighty push and sent her weaving backwards to land with a heavy thud on the dance floor.

The band stopped playing and the crowd stopped jabbering. The atmosphere bristled like a cactus plant. The Mexican woman's black eyes dug into me the way she wished her teeth could.

The boys in the band grabbed me and hid me behind the piano. Just then the owner of the saloon, a hefty man in a fancy-beaded vest, ran over and yanked the woman off the floor, yelling, "You come een my place again you no leave alive! This is las' time you mess around weeth my musicians!"

Whereupon he flung her out through the swinging doors. "Go ahead, boys," he shouted as he went back behind the bar. "She's a no-good! Every night she makes a fuss. I throw her out for good. It's okay, boys! Drinks on the house! Come on, geeve us some jazzy music!"

Everybody laughed and cheered and quickly forgot. But the episode left me shivering. Not until we crossed back over the border late that night did I stop shaking and then I began roaring with laughter with the rest of the boys.

The next day was Sunday. In the morning the girl from the art school called for me in her father's car and we drove out to Point Loma, a peninsula which graces the bay of San Diego. There we painted water colors of the fishermen's wharves and spent a long afternoon talking about art and plans for the future. Oddly enough, they coincided—that is, she also had the bug for the big city, and an especially strong feeling for New York. Even on music we agreed. Her favorite tune was George Gershwin's "Someone to Watch Over Me" and it happened to be mine too.

I refrained from telling her I played in a dance band over the border, as Tia Juana had a bad reputation, and even if she knew I needed the money for train fare to New York she might get the impression I was going to the dogs before getting started.

That evening when we drove back to her house and I met and shook hands with her father, I had to gulp. We had seen each other before: he was the man who managed the music store downtown!

10

FANFARE

*L*IVING ON Hermosa Street gave me just the time necessary to plan and dream of the coming trip—and the girl from the art school. Before she left San Diego for college up north, we parted with a promise to write.

These dreams were augmented by my reading O. Henry's stories, which brought New York right into my room. One night, while imagining I could hear the sound of tugboats on the East River, the loud honking of an automobile horn outside the window brought me back to reality. The boys in the orchestra were signaling me to drive out to a dance job—the last job before taking off for the East. A more fitting finale could not have been arranged.

We drove far out into the country in the rain to a peculiar roadhouse surrounded by squat palm trees. We knew we had reached our destination when a gaudy electric sign wiggled through the wet windshield announcing "Palm Gardens—Dancing—Bring Your Own." Even in the drizzle there seemed to be something familiar about this place. Suddenly, when I caught sight of swings in the rear of the roadhouse, something clicked: this was the very same old schoolhouse to which Mrs. Blass had taken us in her flivver on that sad Sunday picnic years ago!

Playing hot dance music to a drunken clientele in this remodeled schoolhouse aroused thoughts from out of the past. While blowing away on my horn I wondered what Mrs. Blass might be up to on her new walnut orchard in a small upstate town. I thought about Botsford: what had happened to him? Since his father was in the consular service and his parents had reunited, Botsford might be in Arabia or some

56

other distant land. And Hortense—how was she getting along, married to Sylvester, the man Mrs. Blass had picked out for her? My brother Warren was up to his ears in his own guava jelly business somewhere in Florida. My father had been going out on extensive lecture tours with Uncle Ed, who spoke to the schools of the West on his favorite subject: the redwoods. My father made all the arrangements for these lectures and also worked the projection machine which showed slides from his brother's collection of photographs.

When the band struck up the last tune, "Farewell Blues," I felt an omen coming on.

A few days later everything was set; my suitcase was packed and ready, all that remained for me to do was to make a phone call to my grandmother, who was now well again. Having completely forgotten about the problem of getting humble, I was greatly stunned when the subject came up during our telephone conversation. She remarked on the change in my attitude and she went so far as to congratulate me; not only that, she gave me her full consent. Now that I expressed what she called "the true humility," which she said was the *real* me, she announced that I could go to New York or any place I wanted.

Naturally the news was terrific, but she had no idea that I was phoning her from the railroad station and that I had already bought my ticket through to Indianapolis. From there I planned to hitchhike to New York. Nothing could stop me now, not even a final plea from Mrs. Blass.

A letter from her had arrived the day before I boarded the train, the first of a series to come from her hand, still trying to guide and hold me within her exalted daydreams.

My Boy [she wrote], I have just heard a rumor that you are to set out for the East any day. Are you really planning to go all the way to New York? If so I plead with you to take caution and contemplate the straight and narrow way which is the only way you must go, along the lines I have always tried so hard to lead you.

There is just one thing I want you to promise me. When it comes time to consider the right girl you must let me know. This reminds me, when you get to New York (the sound of that place does frighten me, I'll have to admit—are you sure you are ready for this step? Shouldn't you go to college a few years first?) But as I was saying you will look up that lovely girl Ada Staley. She is doing very well in her music I hear, orchestral work I believe. Such a wholesome type. You and she always struck it off so well together, you recall. I will come and visit you if ever you two should become serious enough to contemplate marriage. You can count on my being there for the ceremony. It would be the answer to my prayers, my heart's desire—but then you have your own life to live and I must not try and outline it for you.

Here are a few hints I want you to carry along. A fine handsome upright man of middle age came through here last week and gave a lecture. Oh, how I wished for you then! The enclosed clipping gives excerpts from his talk and I know they will be inspirational pillars of light for you to go by in the dark days ahead. His lecture was titled Character: How to Mold and Hold It.

And now, all my love—

Auntie Carrie

The clipping must have slipped out before she sealed the envelope. I had to leave without the pillars.

PART TWO

11

SKYLINE

ONE STATE after another rolled out its vast earth-green rug under me. I was well on my way at last.

But making a beeline across the map of America took slightly longer than calculated. I had to make a stopover in Indianapolis in order to do a little financial refueling. Picking up a few one-night orchestra engagements gave the needed pecuniary push and then I was ready to hitch a ride the rest of the distance.

Standing on the highway just outside the city limits, I waved a battered trumpet case relentlessly at every moving object to come over the hill heading east. After a good hour of this exercise and with both my thumbs going numb I still had no luck.

During this quiet spell by the roadside I could almost hear myself thinking, it was so peaceful—and if there was anything to be avoided at this stage, it was an examination of my own thoughts.

True, I was now free and on my own for the first time, and yet having so much freedom all at once rather overwhelmed me. I hoped that no one would ask me what I intended doing and exactly what I wanted out of life because I realized one thing while waiting there— I had no clear answer.

61

My mind was a menagerie of desires: I wanted to be an artist, certainly, but I wanted just as much to see New York and find out how everybody lived and how they looked and acted. I wanted to play a horn, too—this was probably the only thing I had a grain of confidence in doing—and along with this I wanted to find out whether or not it was possible to earn a living, at anything. What it came right down to, I suppose, was that I only wanted to live and look around.

Just as long as nobody asked me precisely what I was aiming for!

The best remedy for this sort of self-conscious truth picking is whistling, and that morning I became an expert whistler. The birds around the countryside had a hard time drowning me out, but unfortunately I could conjure up no song which would effectively cheer my spirits. Every tune I started to whistle only added to the general dilemma; tunes like "Me and My Shadow" and "I'm Runnin' Wild" and "Stumblin'" kept coming to the surface.

Finally I let the birds take over.

And yet this wait was well rewarded when a slightly bruised Buick roadster came whizzing over the hill and to my amazement screeched to a dead stop directly in front of where I was waving. A door opened and naturally I hopped in.

Hitching this ride from Indianapolis to the great metropolis came as a break in more ways than one, considering the number of flat tires we experienced, all of which kept me in constant suspense of ever arriving at our destination.

The generous driver, a stubby man with a sawed-off cigar and a special gift of gab, let me know that I was riding with the top Easter-egg-dye salesman for the entire Middle West, a cynical character whose home was in New York. It was then the fall of '29 and he was sailing high on the crest of prosperity and I was only too glad to be accompanying him on his cruise.

"What's the idea of you wanting to come all the way from a beautiful state like California to New York for?" was almost his first question. And right off he had me stumped. No answer I could think of could possibly satisfy such a practical and hard-boiled businessman.

But I wanted to be friendly, so I said, "Well, I've just got to go, that's all."

62

He twisted his cigar to the other corner of his mouth. "Yeah, but still I can't understand why the likes of you should ever want to come to a crowded place like New York. I've been living there for twenty-two years and that's twenty-two years too long, if you ask me."

"What's the matter with it?" I did ask.

"Oh, hell, it's too damn full of people what come from some place they ought to go back to," he said.

"Like me, you mean?" I had to say.

"Well, not exactly," he said, with a sly look in his eye, insinuating plainly enough that he meant I was only going to add to the confusion of his already overstuffed city.

"But I guess I've got as much right to go there as anybody," I said, defending my dream. "After all, you came from someplace else origin-ally, didn't you?"

The dye salesman didn't answer this and we drove on for many miles in silence before he spoke again.

"Don't get me wrong, makes no difference to me, it ain't none of my worry, all I say is it's no fairyland, if you're thinking of staying there I'm only warning you they don't trip the light fantastic any more if you've got that notion—say," he interrupted himself, "what line are you in—I mean, what business are you going to try to work yourself into?"

"I'm going to try to be an artist."

"Holy cats!" he roared. "Ain't there enough starving artists in the world already?" This crack stopped conversation for a while.

During the ensuing lull I considered easing his concern about me by telling him that he needn't get upset; actually I had ample assurance of setting foot on Manhattan Island without the worry of finding work. A hunk of luck came my way in Indiana. Playing those handy one-night stands resulted in my meeting an exceptionally kindhearted trombone player who at that time was sliding his way west from New York. That we were brothers in brass proved most helpful. Without letting me know, he had sent a stream of persuasive telegrams to his Broadway booking agent and in very short order succeeded in securing for me the promise of a job playing in a ship's orchestra. The exact particulars regarding the ship's destination remained obscure, but this hardly mattered since I knew the important detail that the cruise was set for the first of October.

I pondered the advisability of explaining all this to my skeptical friend but decided not to say a word. He was fretful enough about my becoming a starving artist without any reference to the prospects of my becoming a poverty-stricken musician to boot.

In the early morning of the second day, the salesman nudged me out of a short dream. "Hey, kid, there's your city up ahead!" he said, and he wasn't fooling.

64

Far off in the hazy distance the delicate skyline of New York pointed its slender fingers into the dawn. In the faint morning light the city still seemed like a mirage luring us on mile after mile when bang! the third and toughest tire of the set celebrated by blowing out. The salesman drew over to the side of the highway, swearing a light-blue streak as we climbed out.

"Of all places to have a flat—in the middle of these dumpy Jersey meadows!" he stormed, taking off his coat and getting out the jack. The city by now was close enough to be almost believable. The jagged skyscrapers took on solid dimensions and I could begin imagining people living in the buildings. I started making a quick drawing of my first impression of the city on a piece of paper which I pulled from my pocket.

The salesman yelled up at me from under the rear axle, "Hey, Rembrandt, how's about giving me a hand with this damn tire! There'll be plenty of time for you to make sketches when you get there but first we gotta get out of here!"

The car was quickly jacked up and the tire fixed and we were off for the final miles. Soon only the Hudson River lay between us and the city. Then a ferryboat carried its anxious cargo across the river and we streamed off in a fast lane of traffic and I was on Manhattan Island at last!

"All right, here we are!" said my generous friend. "So now where do you want to be left off at?"

Instead of just saying anyplace, which certainly would have been the polite thing, I asked him if he happened to be driving anywhere near the Metropolitan Museum of Art.

"Sure thing," he said, "I pass by the Met right on my way to the Bronx. But you can't get a room and bath in there!"

As he steered the car through the jammed streets and wide avenues I craned to see all the sights from the window. As we drove through the garment district where men and boys pushed carts loaded with colorful clothing, the salesman began popping with civic pride. "This here's the garment center where they make all the women's dresses and men's clothes. I'll bet that there suit you're wearing came from right around here someplace!"

A few blocks later he motioned to the left. "And there's our famous Metropolitan Opera House."

"You mean that old building?" I said, not meaning to insult him, though to me it looked just like a huge brick icehouse.

"Just wait till you see the insides," he snapped. "The Diamond Horseshoe ain't nothing to sneeze at, brother!"

The swift trip up Fifth Avenue to the museum was filled with a million impressions of endless crowds wearing unfathomable facial expressions.

"Where's everybody going, and what's the big rush?" I asked. "And why do they all look so darn worried?"

"Don't ask me, my friend. I've been here twenty-two years and I've never been able to figure it out. That's a little project I leave for you to solve."

I seriously and secretly accepted this "project" and determined to find the answer even if it took me twenty-five years.

As the salesman let me off in front of the Metropolitan Museum he shook my hand and said, "Whatever it is you're after, kid, I hope you find it. Good luck!" Then he drove away in a cloud of cigar smoke.

Inside the cool museum I checked my suitcase and trumpet and walked reverently through the vast halls, slowly becoming lost in the silent centuries, exploring the Egyptian tombs, the beauty of the Greek temples, and moving on up through the ages until I came face to face with Rembrandt. I stood astonished before his self-portrait—

how could it be?—Rembrandt looked exactly like the Easter-egg-dye salesman!

Then on to the other masters, Rubens, El Greco, Goya, and Van Gogh. Not until I came upon a painting of a dust storm on Fifth Avenue by John Sloan did I realize what century it was. Four o'clock and time to get going.

12

PAGEANT

SOMEHOW I managed to locate the Broadway booking office, the address of which I had on the letter written by the trombonist back in Indianapolis. I handed the letter of introduction to the officious girl at the front desk. She read the contents and then looked up.

"I'm sorry but that cruise to South America has been canceled," she said.

"Canceled?" I choked.

"Yep," she said, as she put on her glasses and returned to her typewriter.

For a few seconds I just stared into space not knowing what to say next. The girl said nothing.

I must be sympathetic with her, I thought to myself. I must realize that for years she has been telling stray out-of-town musicians that their cruises have been canceled and she's probably learned not to get too worked up over individual cases although inside she must be tearing herself apart emotionally. I sat down on the waiting-room bench with a couple of other dejected characters. I thought there might be a possibility of her speaking to me again.

It could just happen that she would remember about a trumpet player needed on some other ship, say, for instance, one going to Europe. I had nothing against going to Europe. But she didn't come through with any such inspiration. Finally I left the office.

Dazed at finding myself unexpectedly without a job and yet more than a little dazzled at having landed at last in New York, I stood on the corner of 47th Street and Broadway holding my horn in one hand and my suitcase in the other. From the open windows above came

68

sounds of saxophones, pianos and trombones. This, I knew instinctively, was Tin-Pan Alley!

Large gold lettering on the windows announced the names of famous as well as struggling song pluggers. Imagine my excitement at seeing W. C. Handy's name on one of the windows—the father of the blues! Someday I would have the nerve to go see him and shake his hand. Through the din I could hear the strains of a current tune emanating from Irving Berlin's publishing offices; a sad saxophone wailed "All Alone."

Now part of the milling musicians jamming the sidewalks, I gawked at the passing show. Several times while standing wide-eyed I was pushed off the curb and into the street, only to be pushed back again by the taxis streaking by.

"So what?" I said, half to myself and half to whom it might, but certainly didn't seem to, concern. "So I'm stranded in New York and isn't this where I've always wanted to be?" I was unable to answer.

On the sidewalks oily-haired musicians maneuvered around dressed in broad-shouldered, snappy, striped suits with wide bell-bottomed pants. This doggy attire, together with their cargo of instruments, took up considerable space and made walking difficult and standing around hazardous.

A policeman appeared, the signal for all loitering musicians to keep moving, and I was swept into the maelstrom.

69

Times Square before showtime

While drifting along with the musical crew I started talking to a friendly E-flat alto player. He saw right away that I was new to the Street and he offered me the lowdown on how to go about getting a job. Being one of the boys who lived in the night smoke of dance halls and night clubs blowing his lungs out, he knew the ropes.

The men who booked bands for dance dates, he explained, hired their combinations right there on the sidewalks. It was understood that any musician seen hanging around was more or less available for work. He tipped me off that the trick was to look "all booked-up" and in demand.

"That is," he added, "if you want a high-class job. They never sign you if you look dumpy and out of circulation. By the way," the dapper sax man continued, "you could sure do with a new suit or some shoulder pads to bring out your personality. You'll be mistook for a dopey out-of-towner the way you're dressed now."

"I'll try to get a tailor to build me up," I said.

"Well, keep drapin' yourself around this district, bud," he ended encouragingly. "You'll scoop a date yet—that is, if yer hot. Sweet stuff don't go so good these days."

"Thanks a lot," I said. "I'll keep trying."

So with my horn for bait I started cruising the West Forties. Now I was in the same boat as the others. I found I was wearing the same worried expression I had seen that morning on the crowd. Maybe I had already begun to find the answer to the project!

By seven o'clock, dirty and dog-tired, I decided to call it quits and I checked into a small hotel off Broadway. After cleaning up and attempting a quick snooze I went out again for a bite to eat and to take in the Great White Way at night.

Broadway by this hour was going full-flare with its glaring electrical aurora borealis flooding the faces in the crowds.

What a stupendous eyeful! Here on these wide sidewalks an endless advancing multitude swept along in passionate pursuit of pleasure. The greatest wonder of all lay in the fact that every face was designed differently. No stock pattern had been used; each was an original, created from the many nations that have made New York's population. Feeling as if the whole pageant had been put on especially for me, I

72

stood soaking up the stream of passing history. Much as I wanted to take in all the brilliance that one night, some had to be left for the following few years.

Hardly aware of it at the moment, I had set sail on a round-the-world trip of my own launching, and the extent of this tour was to be the circumference of Manhattan Island.

Back in the hotel room I sank onto the sagging bed and watched the red glow from the Broadway signs flash on and off against the wall. Warmed by the sights of the day and by the realization that the long drawn-out dream had at last materialized, I now began longing for the day when I could send for the girl in California.

Superimposed over the thousands of faces I had seen that day, hers shone out distinctly. She must come and share the wealth of this rich new territory I had discovered, that is, as soon as I had learned the trick of how to make a living here myself. That night I wrote a short letter to her describing (mostly by exclamation marks) the happenings of this first day.

But the day was not over—not quite yet.

From the next room voices persisted in penetrating through the thin partitions and kept me from going to sleep. Two people, a man and a woman, were unmistakably arguing. Their voices would be furious one minute and then die down to a whisper the next. I strained my ears to hear.

As the argument continued, the man yelled at the top of his hoarse voice, "If you told Ferris about my plans, so help me I'll slug you!"

Then came the distressed voice of the woman pleading, "I didn't tell him! Believe me, I didn't! Let go, you're hurting me!"

Scared stiff, I sat up perspiring, with one ear pressed to the wall.

"I'll kill you, by God, I'll kill you!" the man shouted. "You know damn well you squealed on me!"

Next came a sudden violent commotion. Something heavy fell to the floor and a bottle crashed against the thin wall. I jumped out of bed and grabbed the phone. I shouted frantically to the hotel manager, "Somebody hurry up here and do something! A women is being murdered in the next room!"

A few paralyzing minutes passed. There was only desperate silence

73

from the next room. I was terrified. Had I called for help too late? There was a knock at my door. A Hawaiian bellhop handed me a pitcher of ice water.

"No worry yourself," he said, smiling. "No harm. You only hear actors rehearsing for show. I tell them be more quiet. Hotel full of actors, dancers, musicians. All make crazy noise. But you no worry yourself. Hardly ever murder in this hotel—only once since I work here. Thank you. Good night."

13

TIN-PAN ALLEY

THE NEXT morning I looked out the window. The city was still there but considerably calmed compared to the wild night before. Since it was too early for the musicians and band bookers to be on the pavements, I decided to locate the Art Students' League, where I planned to study. It is not far from Tin-Pan Alley, only ten blocks. Everything in the city seemed surprisingly compact: Rembrandt only a nickel away from the Paramount Building, the Metropolitan Opera right alongside the garment center, and everybody in the whole wide world walking up and down Broadway!

Light as a feather and forgetful of being without a job, I ran up to the League on 57th Street. I was elated to find that John Sloan, whose paintings had thrilled me only the day before at the Metropolitan Museum, was teaching there. The possibility of studying under him was incentive enough to send me back down to Broadway determined to reap enough cash for the tuition fees.

The rest of the day was spent pacing around Tin-Pan Alley. Eventually the hunt proved fruitless. Holding that "booked-up" look became difficult and my situation grew desperate. Finally, after a week, and just as I was about to take a job as a waiter in a Schrafft's restaurant (where I would at least be *near* food), I got a break.

After spotting my horn, a greasy-looking, slick-haired, double-breasted band booker breezed up to me: "Whaddya play, kid, hot or sweet?"

"Mostly hot," I said.

"What style ya dish it out in, Dixieland or Chicago?"

"San Diego style, I guess you'd call it."

"Yer from California? Well, whaddya know? I come from L.A. myself!"

"You don't say!" I exclaimed, and we shook hands. It was good meeting someone from Los Angeles, even if he was slightly greasy.

"Ya workin'?" he asked.

As calmly as possible and tenaciously hanging onto my booked-up look, I answered, "When?"

"Tonight," he said. "I gotta big job for a small combination. It's a radio job and I need a hot trumpet. How about it?"

"Sure!" I caved in.

"Then show up at the Webster Hotel, ninth floor, at eight tonight, meet the boys, and we'll run through a few standard numbers. I want to hear that San Diego style of yours. You might fit in regular with the unit. The radio job don't start till ten, so get with it, eh, kid?" We pumped hands again and said so long.

At eight sharp I walked into the Webster Hotel with my pants newly pressed. The lobby was full of people who looked like permanent transients. A relaxed elevator jogged up to the ninth floor. The sound of a clarinet led me to the right room. The slick band leader opened the door and immediately introduced me to the boys in his band and their girl friends.

The orchestra leader suggested we tune up. His clarinet sounded the A note. I got out my horn and we all tuned up. Soon the room filled with A notes, and the girls joining in vocally.

"Okay, okay! Let's ride into 'Dinah,' boys!" the leader yelled.

Now this was duck soup for me. The tune "Dinah" and I had been friends all across the continent. When it came time for me to swing into a chorus I gave it everything. I caught the leader giving the

75

sax man a wink, so I concluded that I must be satisfactory. Six choruses of "Dinah" and we stopped.

"Okay, we don't need any more workout. If you can read the spots you've got the job," he told me.

Here in the greatest city in the world I was already set in a band! The leader woke me from my daze.

"Hey, can you read the spots—the notes?"

"Sure," I said confidently. "I can even read flypaper."

This wisecrack from the hinterlands fell a little flat and the girls used it as their cue to exit. They unwound themselves from their musician friends.

"Where are you going?" I asked sheepishly.

"We're dancin' in the *Scandals* and we were supposed to be in the dressin' room ten minutes ago. Glad to have met yuh, honey. Be seein' yuh!"

I said thanks, relieved to know they weren't leaving on my account. The chorus danced out and the musicians were left alone with band talk.

At ten we went on the air at some small broadcasting station a few blocks away. The radio announcer announced, "Ted Rollins' Tennessee Nighthawks will entertain you with a half hour of torrid tunes from the South."

One of the characters in the band leaned over and whispered, "I never been south of South Ferry!"

Then began the longest half hour I can remember ever living through. This Ted Rollins man signaled me to take one chorus after

another while the rest of the boys clapped their hands to the off-beat rhythm. Their enthusiastic expressions made me wonder at first if my corny style really had something after all. My gosh, was New York a pushover!

We were off the air at last.

"You were molten lava on that chorus of 'I Can't Give You Anything but Love,' kid!" I can remember the band leader saying later as we packed our instruments and got into our coats. Someone had stuck my trumpet case under the piano, and it took me a while to find it. When I looked around I was alone.

"Hey, where's the rest of the gang?" I called to the announcer as he walked out the door. "Where do we get paid off?"

"Don't ask me. I only bark here," he said in his expensive voice.

Furious, I started to chase after the renegades. The elevator was slow in coming so I ran down four flights of stairs to the street.

Broadway was crowded with every sort of human hazard, so I tried some fancy open-field running through the traffic. Finally, racing into the Webster Hotel, I asked the man at the desk if the boys from Room 918 had checked in.

"Checked in?" the clerk glowered at me. "They've checked out! Those fellows don't live here, they just rented the room to rehearse in today. How should I know where they are now?"

The following day I reluctantly decided to have one last fling at picking up a steady job off the sidewalks, intending at the same time to keep an eagle eye out for that greasy guy who had given me the slip the night before. But no luck. As a last resort I wandered into the Gaiety Building on Broadway, five floors packed with small-time sad

theatrical agents. Each floor had nothing to offer but discouragement—except the fifth. Here the door of one of the offices was wide open. Taking this as a sign of cordiality, I walked in.

Inside the stuffy and active office a singing sister act was giving a tryout. The walls were plastered with photographs of faintly famous entertainers; all had autographed their smiling faces to their agent, who at this moment sat talking into a pay phone planted on top of his desk. This must be Al Romero if the name on the door meant anything.

In the middle of his conversation he suddenly stopped and looked up at me—not at me, exactly, but at the trumpet case I was carrying. We eyed each other for a few seconds.

Then, as he held his hand over the phone receiver, he shouted, "Hey, a trumpet! I just now got a call for a trumpet job. Want to work?"

"What's in it?" I asked him, fortifying myself against any further trickery.

"It's a wedding reception at Hennington Hall down on the East Side. Eleven bucks. So I ask you, do you take it or don't you?"

"Sure, but I gotta be guaranteed the eleven," I said.

"Listen, bud, I'm not a sidewalk booker, am I? I'm in this business ten years and in the same spot, ain't that guarantee enough?"

78

"Sign me up," I said. "I'll blast Hennington Hall wide open for you tonight!" Then he hollered back over the phone that he was sending down the best damn trumpet man in town.

This booker, Al Romero, hadn't even asked me to rip out a chorus. He hadn't even asked me if I had ever played at a wedding reception. But the job was in the bag; he really meant it.

That night I played at Hennington Hall, where pomp and pandemonium reigned together. It was difficult for me to keep my eyes on the music. About midnight we played an easy march while all the relatives lined up and kissed the bride and groom. This ceremony took a long time and it tried the patience of the younger generation. Finally the kids broke loose and started a celebration of their own.

All dressed up in tightly fitted pants, neat white collars and black ties, they began running and sliding the entire length of the floor. One imaginative kid discovered a table piled high with cream puffs. Swiftly and silently they organized into two gangs and before anyone could stop them, a violent cream puff war broke out. These delicacies flew through the air and decorated the walls. Then one of them sailed smack into my face as I was blowing away. It was delicious!

14

SIDESHOW

THE NEXT DAY when I dropped in on Al Romero to collect, he told me he had heard about the incident of the cream puff. Somehow this set me in solid with him.

"How would you like to play at a Jewish banquet this Saturday?" he asked.

"Nothing could suit me better," I told him. "Send me out on any kind of job, anyplace, anytime!"

Al never understood my requests for jobs in all the small-time, knock-down-and-drag-out joints. I never told him that in addition to needing the work I wanted to take in all sides of the city.

Riding the elevated trains to and from the dance dates offered the best means of grasping the full size of the city and its perplexing, kaleidoscopic contrasts. As the train wound its snakelike way through the canyons of dismal tenements along the East Side, one could see the towering buildings of Wall Street rising like huge cash registers, each trying to outdo the other, all this in startling proximity to stark poverty.

From the train windows it was possible to look into the tenement apartments bordering the El. Every manifestation of family life exhibited itself freely. What a show for five cents! The people in their small, stuffy rooms seemed to be immune to the relentless rattling of the passing trains and regarded their coming and going as calmly as they would regard the ebb and flow of the sea. Apparently they hardly cared that the El passengers stared in at them or that an artist might be planning to use them as subjects for future paintings. For this was certainly my uninhibited intention.

Also from the elevated I could see below on Grand Street shop window after shop window of satin-draped mannequins displaying bridal gowns, all enveloped in the foreboding shadows of the Bowery. Near by, men sold diamonds from hand to hand on the sidewalks where other men passed who obviously didn't have the price of a bed for the night. Children played cops and robbers underneath the Bridge of Sighs which crossed from the Courthouse to the Tombs prison. The dimly lit second-floor lofts of ancient buildings exposed hundreds of weary girls making artificial flowers to blossom on Easter hats. Passing through the fur district I saw men transporting armloads of silver fox, which flowed over their shoulders creating an undulating ocean of furs.

New York and I were rapidly becoming good friends; in fact, instead of feeling like a stranger I began to feel as if we had known each other all our lives. Everyone was accepted on equal terms, and made you wonder where you'd been keeping yourself. But along with all this felicity went an inescapable obligation. I knew I had to do something in return for the privilege of being a part of such a family. Every-

Movie houses have their exits

The manicure

thing demanded to be recorded, and my great worry was that the dime-store supply of sketchbooks might run out. They seemed to have only a limited stock and I was practically buying them in carloads. They were small, inconspicuous, leather-bound books which looked like text-books. I liked them for that reason. Sketch pads sold in art stores are obviously arty and a menace. Eyes always start bulging, heads twist around, crowds gather, and an artist usually has to give up sketching. It's a natural reaction; even sign painters are bothered by gawkers. I know that if ever I happened to come across an artist sketching I would break my neck to get a look at what he was doing. But curiosity not only kills cats, it kills creation.

That is why these dime-store books gave me the protection I needed. Whenever I started sketching, I pretended to be making out a laundry list or adding up a column of figures, mumbling aloud. This worked fairly well as a distraction, though I knew I couldn't go on mumbling such stuff as "three socks, six shorts, four shirts" forever. Yet I had to keep drawing so as to let the world know what wonderful people I had come across—not only the way they looked, but the way they invented lives for themselves out of nothing: carrying signs, fishing for change through sidewalk gratings, shining shoes, peddling gardenias, selling corsets, plugging song hits, washing windows, sharpening knives. They made the streets a feast for artists.

84

15

EAST-SIDE SONG

THE JEWISH banquet at which Al Romero had signed me to play was on the lower East Side in a hall named Richter's on Rivington Street. Sid, one of the boys in the band, agreed to show me the way to our job which happened to be near his end of town. We met at the Delancey Street station and walked down Orchard Street, which had the appearance of a special holiday, but Sid said things went on like that down there six days out of the week. Both sides of the street were lined with pushcarts filled with wares ranging from pickled herring to pink corsets and the air was thick with pungent smells, shouting vendors, and melancholy Yiddish Victrola music.

The banquet was already under way when we arrived. It overflowed with loud and good-natured fun, and we went right to work adding music. Sid, a large, robust fellow, all but devoured his saxophone every time a tray loaded with savory food was carried past.

The hours went by quickly and at midnight the musicians were invited to join the guests. Once at the table we were in our element. Sid, knowing that most of the items served were new to me, urged me to sample his favorite dish. It was wonderful, complicated stuff. "What do you call it?" I asked him just when he happened to have his mouth full.

"Gefüllte fish!" he choked.

Naturally I thought he was sneezing, so I said "Gesundheit!"

Everybody at the table hastened to explain that gefüllte fish was the name of the dish. It tasted much better than it sounded.

A half hour was spent devastating the banquet table before we realized we were there to make music and not gluttons of ourselves.

After finishing that job, I decided to spend the rest of my life on the lower East Side where there were so many fabulous subjects to draw! But each section of the city now had me pledging my allegiance to it. The next week when I reported to Al Romero, he said he had a Saturday night job down in the toughest end of town.

"It's at the Minnehaha Club around Mulberry Street in Little Italy near Chinatown," he said. "You'll probably get shot at a few times, but if you don't mind a little thing like that, the job's yours. Eight bucks."

I will never forget seeing Mulberry Street for the first time. Fortunately, I came well loaded with sketchbooks, for a festival was actually in progress. Fancy arches of bright yellow lights spanned the streets. Groups of gaily dressed people expressed themselves in warmhearted dancing and singing in the street while others sat leisurely on the sidelines and watched.

I asked a man who was selling eels out of a barrel what the celebration was all about. "All Saints'," he said. "It's All Saints' Day! You never heard?"

Whatever the religious significance might have been, it was hopelessly smothered in the heavy aroma of cheese and bologna. Long lines of carts bordering the sidewalks displayed an assortment of traditional objects, porcelain saints and wax candles together with balls of cheese in every shape and size. The most popular vendor sold oysters on the half shell. In each block a strenuous band blared forth from platforms built on the streets. Buxom singers sent forth their arias into the already odorous night.

Periodically a solemn procession of old women marched through the crowds in white-stockinged feet, carrying tall lighted candles. Little girls, dressed as angels with slightly soiled gold-tinted cardboard wings, ran by their sides. At one point I attempted a drawing of the scene, but too many curious people swarmed around and I had to give up. A considerate, bright-eyed, dapper young boy wearing a striped vest, dotted tie, and a chain with many dangling ornaments across his chest, came up and asked if I wanted to use his family's window, which was on the third floor.

I eagerly accepted his thoughtful invitation. His family was busy celebrating in their small front room and they cordially insisted I join them in a round of wine. The young boy's beaming uncle asked me to

87

Mulberry Street festival

"maka pitch" of his bambino. Everybody got a kick out of my crude sketch, especially the uncle, who tried to have his bambino drink some of the wine to celebrate but the baby knew better. They treated me like one of the family, offering grapes, cheese, and mountains of spaghetti —the whole place was mine!

"You want to see my papa's marionette show?" the bright-eyed boy asked suddenly while I was wrestling with a forkful of spaghetti. Naturally I wanted to see everything, so he led me through a back window onto a roof—a peculiar procedure, but so far that night the boy had proved himself someone to follow. Away from the street noises, the deserted back yards and rooftops in the moonlight seemed like another world. We climbed down onto a one-story building with a large trap door in the middle of the roof.

The boy lifted up the door and asked, "You want to see where papa keeps his marionettes when they aren't acting?"

Down through the opening I could see dozens of magnificently carved figures about two feet high, all clad in brilliant brass and copper armor, hanging limp from their network of strings.

"The show is going on now. Let's go down and see my papa work them."

A long ladder led down to backstage of a miniature theater. The boy's father couldn't have been overlooked as he loomed immense beside the marionettes. His powerful Italian voice shook the walls as

he shouted out the melodramatic dialogue of all the different parts, heroines, heroes and villains, while he and an assistant manipulated the intricate strings.

"We're just in time for the duel scene," the boy whispered as the long swords tied to the actors' tiny wooden hands began slashing at each other in a furious all-out battle.

At the height of this scene I suddenly remembered that I was supposed to be playing in an orchestra at the Minnehaha Club! I was already a half hour late! Leaving the bright and noisy gaiety of Mulberry Street, I hurried through the dark and forbidding lanes of Chinatown. Abruptly, I came upon the most derelict section imaginable. Pitiful figures of men staggered as in a trance through the streets. Rushing on to find the club, I nearly stumbled over the body of a drunken old man lying along the curbing. Other prostrate forms were slumped in the foul doorways. Could this be a nightmare? No, it was the Bowery, the rear exit of human existence, the dead-end district for forgotten men.

Overhead the ceaseless roar of the elevated trains all but smothered the sound of jangling dance music coming from a large second-story window down the street. Tracing the sound, I saw a gaudily lit, flag-decorated entrance. A crowd of young people were streaming in, casting long animated shadows on the side walk as they went. I knew I had found the Minnehaha Club. The sight was almost incredible: such sudden and carefree gaiety in the midst of all this gruesome and death-like dankness.

At the same time, finding the club came as a great relief. Despite everyone's being really dolled up, I couldn't help feeling apprehensive; this appearance of propriety might be only the cool, smooth shell covering a round of live cartridges.

My worries, however, were unfounded. The job that night turned out not to be so rough as Al Romero had led me to expect. Only one slight disturbance occurred. A boisterous member of the Bowery Athletic Club tripped on the fancy ruffle of his partner's long evening dress, fell, and knocked his head through the bass drum. On the whole, the behavior of these tough boys and their sequined companions was beyond reproach. They acted as strait-laced as a bunch of department store floorwalkers and by the time the dance was over and we had packed up our instruments and were ready to head home, I had transferred my apprehension back to the bitter world of the Bowery outside. But by that hour the streets were completely empty. The drunken old men were probably tucked in either in some precinct house or in the Bowery Mission, where I had been told they had to sing hymns for their supper and a cot. These poor, battered old men were on the town, and the town was down on them.

16

EMBERS OF A ROMANCE

*N*OW THAT Al Romero had improved the dance-job situation, the next problem was to find a decent room in which to lay my head and horn. After spending that first night in the hotel where actors rehearsed murders, I slept, or rather tried to sleep, in a rooming house in the West Fifties in the middle of Hell's Kitchen. The window of my stuffy room opened out on the New York Telephone Company building only a few feet away. All through the long nights a constant drone of switchboard operators' voices kept me awake: hundreds of girls all repeating, "What number are you calling, please?" It seemed as if no one in the entire city ever called the right number during my stay there. Each morning, bleary-eyed, I complained to the landlady but it did no good. She had my rent money for the week in advance and she was not concerned.

From out my window late one moonlight night I watched a mother who was like a beautiful madonna nursing her baby as she lay on a mattress out on the fire escape. Her room was probably a suffocating hotbox and she had sought relief outside in the rich velvet darkness.

In the daytime I watched pigeon fanciers release their feathered flocks, and by means of long poles guide their courses. The birds obeyed, swerving around and around overhead only to return obediently to roost after a few minutes of freedom. With all the sky in which to fly, they preferred being cooped up in their small cages on a grimy rooftop, even as millions of people like myself had flocked to the congested city built on a sliver of an island when there were all the measureless areas of land for us to inherit.

Madonna of the fire escape

With the drone of the telephone operators' voices still buzzing in my ears, I must have worn an especially long face when I went out for breakfast after the seventh night. An antique dealer might well have picked me up for some rare old rocking chair as I weaved groggily for the Automat, through armies of work-bound stenographers. On this of all mornings I spied an acquaintance of mine from out of the past! To be sure, in the Automat you were liable to run into anyone—but seldom someone from your home town.

Yet after several minutes of grade A staring, my weary eyes convinced me that they had lit upon, of all people, Ada Staley. With her faithful cello, there she sat only a few tables away near the side wall, reading a newspaper and chewing gum with the concentrated persistence of a riveter. Her large cello case leaned on the empty chair next to her. Here I was, surrounded by millions of new and exciting people, and yet the mere sight of someone from the all but faded past suddenly evoked a glow like the warmth of a blazing fireside, arousing feelings I had no idea existed. All at once she was not just "someone from the past"; she was Ada Staley, grown up, a person, a woman.

Instead of hurrying right over to her table, my conscience checked me. Maybe I ought not to get involved with her. After all, no one *commanded* me to break in on her! But, then, why had it happened this way? The very sight of her sent quivering through my system vibrations which settled mostly around my heart. Until that moment I hadn't realized how awfully lonesome I was; now all the weeks of aloneness suddenly bunched up and clogged my throat.

Could it possibly be fate moving in? By fate I meant, of course, Mrs. Blass; could she have been right all along? Was there truly something deep and sure-to-be between Ada and me which had been resisted through the years?

All at once no one seemed real in the entire Automat but the two of us. I knew then I must go and speak with her. Feeling miserably inept and awkward, I wondered what to say so as not to frighten her. Gulping my coffee I anxiously moved over toward her table. Of the four chairs, she and her cello already occupied two. The others were taken by strangers even stranger than ourselves. With forced casualness I came up behind her.

97

"Young lady, would you mind removing your small child?" I asked, taking her cello case and resting it against the wall. "I would like to use this chair if you don't mind."

Swinging around furiously, she glared at me, then her frown quickly spattered into a mixture of incredulity and delight. "No," she cried, almost swallowing her gum, "it's not *you!*"

"Yep," I admitted.

Our conversation exploded like a string of firecrackers, small chatter about how she thought that I'd be in Paris by now and how I thought that she'd be packing them in at Carnegie Hall.

"And what about Mrs. Blass?" she asked. "Do you ever hear from her? She keeps in touch with my father and he says she's principal of a school up in the northern part of the state and lives on a walnut farm. What's the latest you've heard?"

I didn't have much information to add, only that I knew Mrs. Blass must be despairing of me since I hadn't taken the time to write. Besides, I insisted, she never would have understood what a city does to you, how it opens your eyes to things no one had ever warned you about, how fierce it could be one moment and how friendly the next, and how it forced you to keep on the jump. All this could never be explained in letters to someone living in another world.

Ada agreed. Her trials in the city she had also kept secret, not even letting her father know how tough plowing the music field was or that she had failed to make the grade. She had had time to look over the odds and this helped her decide against becoming a hungry *artiste*. Symphony work was too risky and she realized she hadn't the talent it takes for solo work.

We drank many cups of coffee while she talked and I noticed that her young face seemed harsher than at first. Her getup was a little careless and the powder on her face patchy.

She gave complete vent to her feelings as she continued. "I started going around to the variety agents," she said, "you know, those cheap punks who dish out trio work for dinners and stuff like that. A few of us girls tried forming a unit to play vaudeville. Not much encouragement there but we hung together. When times got too tough we answered an ad from a commercial firm asking for girls to take laboratory tests. You know, testing different brands of food and cosmetics, which

have to pass a medical code or something like that. They have to find out if the stuff is poisonous or not. The pay was okay—at least it got us by for another few weeks without worrying over our rent. But it wasn't easy."

She paused a second, and then went on: "Maybe I oughtn't to be telling you this, but now that I'm not doing it any longer it kind of seems crazy and almost funny when I look back. Well, anyway, you won't be too shocked if I tell you that I finally had to take a job in the chorus line of a burlesque, will you?"

Before I had a chance to be shocked I shrugged it off.

"Well, when all my savings gave out it was the only job my agent could get me," she said, taking me further into her confidence. "Nobody will ever know how tough it was that first day on stage—my father back home thinking I was playing in some great symphony while there I was exposing everything Mother Nature gave me in front of a bunch of lugs!"

Here I had to break in; I resented being called a lug. In an over-earnest attempt to make her feel better I told her that I'd been to burlesque shows several times—and made many drawings there.

"You mean to say you see art in those shows?" she asked.

Although it happened to be partly true, I didn't expect her to believe it. I'd gone to see them sometimes, bluffing myself that it was a good substitute for art school, a real life class where I could study anatomy in action.

"Well, it ain't art from where I stood!" she said bitterly. "I fainted the first day after playing four shows—I'd only had a glass of milk for lunch."

"But at least it's being a part of show business," I said, with a fine mixture of sympathy and stupidity. Nothing would come out of my mouth the way I intended.

"Oh, don't worry," she said. "It lasted only a few weeks and it cured me. I'll never forsake my cello again. Things are better now, though," she added lightly. "At least we've landed something solid. Tomorrow we'll be going out on the first turn of the 'Wheel'—that's what they call playing the jerk-town circuit around the country. It'll be fun playing in an all-girl orchestra."

My ears welcomed these words of dubious cheer and I was encouraged to ask a question in order to settle something. "How about all your boy friends? Aren't they going to miss you?"

"Boy friends? Oh, *those!* They don't bother me and I'm not going to bother them. So that's that. By the way," she added, "do you remember how Mrs. Blass used to try and get us to go steady?"

We smiled at this dead subject, the remains of a lovesick dream which lingered only in the mind of someone far away, someone who was probably blissfully picking walnuts at that moment.

Ada said that she had to report to a rehearsal hall on 49th Street and added, "It's not Big Time, you know, but we expect to *have* a pretty big time."

"Oh, well, big time, small time—who cares as long as we're busy?"

"Keep busy is right," she said, putting her instrument under one arm and speaking as if I were merely a musician friend she'd seen every day. "Well, I've got to blow now. But wait a minute . . ." she stopped abruptly. "Did you say you were still looking for a decent place to live?"

100

I rendered her a picture of my room-renting trouble. With a brightness that made her look the way she had at the age of nine, she said, "Well, why can't you take my room downtown in Greenwich Village? It's near Sheridan Square, first local stop after Fourteenth Street. I had one hell of a time getting a place. A social worker at the Greenwich Settlement found it for me. It's not much but it's quiet and large enough for you and your trumpet."

"Honest?" I shouted. "Where? When?"

Her words chased each other like ducks in a shooting gallery. "This afternoon I was going to hand the key back to the landlord. I haven't told him yet that I'm leaving but the rent's paid and you can have the place if you want it. Here's the key. We're leaving around eight-thirty, so the room will be empty tonight. Here." She wrote down the address on the back of an envelope and handed it to me.

All I could say was, "Thanks, Ada, thanks a lot. And lots of luck." We shook hands and then she went whirling through the revolving door and disappeared in the crowd.

For several minutes the strong grasp of her hand lingered in mine. It was a hand at once vigorous, friendly and firm, and I felt proud to have known her. She wasn't weak. Not once had she allowed me to take pity on her plight. Underneath her hardened exterior I knew there burned a flame of unquenchable determination. In all the excitement of encountering a page from my past—to say nothing of my new room— I sat down again and drank up the half-empty cup of coffee. If I didn't propose a silent toast to Ada at this moment, I should have, for she saved the day for me.

Freedom of the Press

17

HORN-OF-PLENTY TROUBLE

*T*HAT NIGHT immediately after blowing the last note in the last chorus, I frantically packed my trumpet and left the rest of the boys wondering what had hit me. Why should any of them be expected to understand what it was like getting a room in Greenwich Village from a girl who once lived on a lemon farm in Escondido, California, and who now had come to my rescue in New York—I didn't understand it myself.

I dashed to my old room in Hell's Kitchen. I threw all my clothes and drawing materials into a suitcase, said good-bye out the window to the telephone operators, and then ran all the way to the subway station.

For that hour of the night the subway train seemed unusually crowded. Everybody carried newspapers with blazing headlines and when I finally found a seat, I began reading over someone's shoulder. It *was* big news. STOCK MARKET CRASHES! the thick letters shouted. I had been so busy crashing myself that this terrible catastrophe almost passed me by. Formal and fancily dressed people from the midnight movies sat alongside rugged, overalled men going to work; everybody read the news, their eyes glued to the print. The tragic look on the faces of the readers startled me: each looked as if he had lost at least a million with the market's nose dive. Expressions ranging from shock and surprise to cold, resigned indifference showed plainly on their faces.

At every stop an entirely new cast of characters entered the train and added their frustration to the drama. I started making sketches on the back of some music sheets. Never before had I seen such a gathering. Every kind of character, every color and shade of humanity was represented there.

While engrossed in drawing one of the passengers sitting opposite me, the subway jerked suddenly to a stop. I glanced up. It was Sheridan Square—my station! The air-compressed doors opened quickly; I grabbed my suitcase and ran out. Just as I stepped onto the platform I knew something was missing. It was my horn—my living!

I turned to rush back into the car when the automatic doors shut emphatically in my face. As the windows streaked by I tried to catch a passenger's eye, any passenger's, but they all sat motionless with their washed-out, vacant stares.

When I pulled my senses together I ran through the turnstile and yelled to the man in the change booth. "Hey, mister, my horn! I left it on the train that's pulled out!"

He didn't move a muscle. He only said, "Your *what?*"

"My horn, my trumpet! I'm a musician. Will you phone to the next station and tell them to get it for me, please?"

His placid expression began to change; it slid into a cold smile. "Phone?" he said. "Take it easy, bud. Take it easy!"

"Well, what can you do to get it for me?" I screamed.

"Listen, kid," he said, "you'd just better say good-bye to your trumpet. You'll never see it again. Not a chance."

"What?" I shouted, as if he had stolen it. "At the end of the line it'll still be there! I can't afford to lose it!"

"Don't get so worked up, bud," he said. "You only lost a horn! What about all them people what lost millions of dollars today in the stock market crash? They really got something to bellyache about!"

A line of people started forming behind me. The man in the booth became impatient. "Listen, kid, don't you see you're holdin' up traffic? I'm tellin' you, you're wastin' your time, and mine too!"

He meant what he said and I stepped aside. I had never thought how it would feel to be without my trumpet. It was a terrible sensation, like having had my closest friend run out on me.

I hunted crazily through the jigsaw puzzle of Greenwich Village till I finally found my new room on a dark narrow street. It turned out to be no larger than a flute case but it was quiet. I threw down the suitcase and the bundle of sheet music and sat on the edge of the bed, befuddled. The scattered sketches of the subway passengers stared up at me from the floor. Which one of them was now in possession of my horn? They all began to look like potential villains.

Something made me wonder if losing my horn might not be some sort of omen—one of Mrs. Blass's omens. Hadn't I forgotten the horn because I was so absorbed in drawing? I resolved to be an artist for fair; the next day I would go to Wall Street, see the panic firsthand, make a drawing and sell it to a newspaper.

Somewhat comforted by this new plan, I decided to get to bed and stop worrying. When I leaned down and opened the suitcase, spots suddenly appeared before my eyes—big, black spots!

There inside the suitcase on my shirts and socks were fresh stains of India ink. During the rush to the subway the stopper on my ink bottle had loosened and the indelible drawing ink had oozed out. Worst of all, a letter from my girl in California was completely blotched! I slammed down the lid, pulled out the light, and went to sleep with my clothes on.

After having so foolishly and generously contributed my horn to someone on the Seventh Avenue subway, I searched every pawnshop on the West Side hoping it would turn up. The more I hunted for the horn the more I grew determined to be an artist. This conviction could hardly have been considered momentous since every day I had made innumerable scribbles dealing with the life all around, but the fact that I was now determined to find some way of earning a living by this scribbling was the new twist that would keep me awake nights. Immediately I set to work creating jokes and inking them in.

First I tried being generous to the editors of the barbershop brand of magazines, such as *Judge* and the old *Life,* giving them the opportunity of selecting and printing several of my things. To my astonishment these czars of the bazaar all found the work completely resistible. At first I failed to understand just what punch my cartoons lacked. Much later the reason for this discrepancy came to the surface: my heart was simply not in the funny-bone yard. How could a guy be expected to cook up gags when he'd just lost the best horn he'd ever had?

But before I realized that this was the trouble I stirred up nerve enough to go into the more sophisticated magazine field. The *New Yorker* was a modest publication in those days and so I approached it very modestly. I thought I would hand the editors only one joke at a time and make them cry for more. An artist acquaintance informed me that every Tuesday was the day to submit ideas and drawings.

109

The sketch I submitted was of two rather tough kids hanging onto the rear end of a taxi which was tearing through traffic. One kid says to the other, "Jeez, Louie, don't you hope dey go clean to Allen Street?" That's all there was to it. *"Jeez, Louie, don't you hope dey go clean to Allen Street?"* The next Tuesday, when I called at the office to find out how the idea had gone over, I was told that the editors were interested and wondered if I could sketch it over again in another shape, rectangular instead of oblong, and then let them see it again.

I worked a solid week on that one subject, doing it over and over until I ran out of paper and patience. The following Tuesday I handed it in and waited another week for an answer. They had a few concrete suggestions this time about the drawing itself. The shape seemed to be all right. One of the editors thought that maybe it would be better if Park Avenue were more readily identifiable.

Back in my low-ceilinged room where the leaky radiator whistled *La Traviata* all day, I took the well-worn drawing and drew in Park Avenue as best I could and promptly and breathlessly brought it back to the girl at the reception desk. A week went by before hearing from them. Then they wrote me a terse letter which hadn't the slightest suggestion of their famous humor; they merely thanked me for submitting the sketch, which they had finally found unacceptable.

Not that I cared to let them off easy, but by that time I actually didn't get the point of the joke either. It had just lit on me one day when I wasn't looking and stuck. I still don't see why I was so worked up, but at first I sure thought it was the greatest idea that ever plagued an editor.

With a large backlog of rejected cartoons, I now had something substantial to show around. The shop windows along Fifth Avenue always intrigued me and I thought possibly one of these stores might be able to use my work. Fall was in the air and so were footballs, and one or two of my cartoons happened to be right in season. The window dresser at Spalding's Athletic Store decided he could use a few slapdash cartoons for his backgrounds. He said he liked my free-for-all style. I believe he thought I had evolved this manner of drawing after years of study. In any case, the fulldressed window with furious football players poster-painted on the backgrounds must have scared the customers away because the job lasted only that one week. And the necessity of

110

earning a living still stared at me and with my last bit of cash I bought another trumpet on the time-payment plan, the most painless way.

Things were very slow at the time with Al Romero. Hour after hour, day after day, I hung around his crowded booking office waiting for another dance engagement. One day, as I was sitting on the wide window ledge studying the river of humanity streaming down Broadway, Romero's telephone rang.

"How would you like to play a steady job three nights a week—Friday, Saturday and Sunday?" Al Romero asked me.

"Sure thing," I said, jumping off the window ledge and grabbing my trumpet case before he changed his mind.

"Okay, you've got a steady date at the Club El Graucho in Greenwich Village down where all the zany artists hang out. That's the only drawback to the job but the pay's strictly okay."

Al had no idea he was talking to a Village artist in embryo and I intended keeping quiet.

111

"The job starts Saturday," Al said, "and you've got to be fitted for a costume!"

To celebrate the steady job I ran out of the office to my favorite institution, the Automat, and inserted two nickels in the slot for a dish of baked beans. I had practically lived there during those last lean weeks. The practice of eating regularly at the Automat I considered equal to taking a course at the best university. The food was good and the food for thought was even better; as for artists, the Automat was a priceless atelier. Where could you get better models to sit for you or more spacious windows to see by?

Sitting at practically every table there was sure to be some fabulous person willing and eager to share his experiences and spill his philosophy of life. Cab drivers, one-time millionaires, two-timing women, and people from every possible profession came and discussed their problems. I remember wishing that the world could be like the Automat. If everybody could just get together over a cup of coffee every now and then!

18

THE LAUNDRYMAN

*T*HE CLUB El Graucho was conveniently located around the corner from my new room in the Village. The street on which I lived is probably the shortest street in the entire city, but more went on within its brief span than in ten full-size blocks put together. It boasted of a feather pillow factory, a wine distillery, a porcelain saint manufacturer, a barbershop, and a tailorshop. And near by there were Mr. Lebrun and his small French Hand Laundry.

Mr. Lebrun's radio perpetually offered the best in classical music programs. In his shop he ironed out not only his customers' laundry but

also the world's problems, to the accompaniment of the radio. The first morning I went to his shop he was humming an intricate passage from a symphony.

"Listen to this!" he said to me as I deposited my laundry bag. "Listen to the violins, the way they're talking to each other!"

With one hand he simulated conducting the symphony and with the other he continued ironing. During the broadcast an oboe muffed a solo so badly that Mr. Lebrun almost scorched a pair of pajamas. Evidently he knew every note of the complex instrumentation, and he demanded perfection.

"What symphony are they playing?" I asked.

"The last movement of Brahms' Third," Mr. Lebrun said, surprised at my ignorance. He did a superb job of conducting and I felt like applauding when the movement was over.

Mr. Lebrun's shaggy pup stood by his side as if waiting its turn to be put through the wash. On the wall hung a bas-relief of Millet's "Angelus" and a copy of *War and Peace* rested on the shelf with the laundry slips. I was very impressed by my laundryman. To me, even his French accent bespoke Art.

The first day he came up to my room to collect laundry I was very excited. As he sat down to catch his breath after climbing the stairs, he looked around and exclaimed at the number of drawings scattered everywhere.

"I didn't know you were trying to be an artist," he said, picking up one or two of the sketches and scrutinizing them like a true connoisseur. "I thought you were a cornet player."

"Well, I play the horn only as a means to an end," I said. "What I really want to be is an artist but so far it hasn't panned out that way."

He continued examining one of the drawings sketched in the subway and then he shrugged his shoulders, a gesture that could have meant any number of things.

"What do you think of it?" I asked him anxiously.

"I don't like to criticize. People shouldn't criticize if they don't know much about art. *Music* I know something about."

Regardless of his reluctance to say anything about the sketches, Mr. Lebrun must have sensed that I wanted very much to have his opinion.

"How many Beethovens are there?" he said. "I don't think everybody who makes a scribble at two years of age should be an artist. Like the other day, one of my customers tells me I should come see his baby girl how she plays the piano already. He says, 'She's just three years old and she plays only on the black keys.' So she's a genius! He says, 'The black keys are sharps and flats, she won't have anything to do with the ordinary white keys. Anybody can play on the white keys!'" Then Mr. Lebrun added quickly, "Maybe you need to study."

Whether this was sharp criticism or mild encouragement I was unable to tell, but I hastened to add that my intention was to study art as soon as possible. Mr. Lebrun already had another drawing in his hands. His eyes gleamed for a second and then they contracted into an agonized squint. He made no comment and there ensued a few moments of thick silence.

"Well, have you got your wash ready?" he said, finally breaking the tension. "I'd better be on my way. Five more stops to make this morning. Good-bye and good luck," and he went down the stairs with my laundry bag slung over his shoulder.

A few days passed and I still wondered what Mr. Lebrun really thought of my work. Needing encouragement almost as much as a clean shirt, I casually strolled into his shop one evening, hoping that he might feel free to say what he thought. As usual, the radio was tuned to a symphonic program. When Mr. Lebrun saw me he began reminiscing about the time he lived in Paris and the hours he had spent studying the paintings in the Louvre.

116

"There is where you find the real thing! Every painting a master-piece!" he exclaimed. "You should see them, my friend!"

Now I knew what was coming and I was sorry I had shown him my feeble renderings. We negotiated about a freshly ironed shirt and then I started toward the door, not daring to press him for further criticism.

"Maybe I shouldn't say anything to you, my friend," he said hesitatingly, "but after seeing your work I can't help but say that you have a long way to go."

Placing his hot iron to one side, he paused to see how I was reacting. He must have seen how I wanted every word.

"Well, then, I'll tell you without pulling the punch, as they say. Maybe you should take up some other line. Maybe you should stick to your music."

Mr. Lebrun had never heard me play! The punch landed. He returned to his ironing.

I began to feel like a shirt that had just been squeezed through his wringer, my spirit seemed to be dangling limp along with the shirts hanging overhead. I started to leave.

"When do you want me to pick up your wash? Mondays?" he called out.

"Sure, sure! Mondays will be fine," I called back, greatly relieved to know that at least he hadn't given me up completely.

The day before Christmas I got a letter from Mrs. Blass. I remember feeling dismally lonesome and lowdown that day. On top of that, the radiator didn't work. Payments on the horn, rent, food, and the cost of art materials left me broke most of the time. Then too, Mr. Lebrun's long-standing laundry bill was worrying me as much as the fact that he hadn't liked anything I had painted. Then the following letter arrived:

Dearest Boy,

I am so very grateful to Ada Staley for sending me your address. Oh, I do want to know all about you, what you are really doing in your Art, and exactly how hard a time my boy is having. I do so wish I might ease things up for you. I just can't now. Do take a little

117

while to write me, won't you, and talk to me just as you would talk if here.

It is lovely here, sunny, warm during the day. Walnut crop was nothing to speak of this year, twenty-eight sacks. But I got four hundred dollars raise at school and it all evens up.

Here's a thought I received lately, I pass it on to you. Love money—this creates it! So love anything and you will cause it. That which you are trying to acquire, like money or anything else, is not one thing and you another, but you are both. Love money—get the *sense* of it in the bank, in your pocket. You need it to see the world. Don't say that you want enough of it to meet your present needs but sense all you can of it. Your world needs to be seen. You need money in abundance. Don't spend foolishly the little you have until you sense more. Money is not the root of all evil but pride, selfishness and love of so-called human power are the evils and this creates the desire for money that would be used wrongly. If you attach happiness to mere money as money and then lose it, you lose your happiness.

This thought was given me last week by a man who has proved it. He came through here. My darling, I love you so much and am interested in your every move. If my cousin Meggs of Cos Cob, Connecticut, asks you to come to Sunday dinner, do go and take your music. She has such a grand estate. Merry Christmas, and lovingly,

Auntie Carrie

I answered that I appreciated her continuing concern and Yuletide greeting, and that I was finding the city a richly rewarding experience with a wealth of drawable material. As for her advice about "sensing" money in the pocket and in the bank, I said that perhaps it might be easier out in California but it just didn't work that way here in the city. All I could sense in my pockets was a deplorable emptiness.

I didn't hear from her again for a long, long while.

19

NEW YEAR'S EVE

THE COSTUMES were the only annoying feature about the steady job at the Club El Graucho; the manager insisted that we dress as Parisian Apaches. Sitting there playing in blue, bell-bottomed corduroy pants, yellow blouses, red sashes, and black French berets, we looked foolish, but this garb created the Greenwich Village atmosphere his customers expected and willingly paid for.

After the disastrous stock market crash it was impossible to understand why anyone wanted to celebrate New Year's Eve. Half the populace was out looking for that corner around which prosperity was said to be waiting, while the other half stood bewildered on the streets selling apples. Nevertheless, there were still plenty of people left with enough money to celebrate frantically. For musicians it was just another night, only louder and longer.

At the management's request we five Apaches arrived earlier than usual at El Graucho that New Year's Eve in order to receive instructions about the pieces we were to play at midnight. I was early so I started sketching our piano player.

The manager, a good guy except for his idea of having us dress as leftovers from the Latin Quarter, noticed me. "I see you like to draw," he said, breathing heavily over my shoulder. "Speaking of artists, we have a reservation tonight for a famous big-time illustrator. Maybe you know him."

When the affable manager mentioned the artist's name, my mouth dropped open. "He's *only* my favorite illustrator!" I said. "You mean *he's* coming in here tonight?"

"Yep, he sure is. This is his reservation right here," and the manager showed me the artist's name on a long list of reservations. "Why so excited? You know him?"

"Well, not exactly," I said, "but I know his work. I used to study his illustrations in the San Diego library by the hour. He sure has a terrific technique!"

"Well, I'll have you meet him when he comes in tonight. Maybe he can give you a break," the manager promised. "We're old friends."

Nothing could have sent in the New Year on better terms with me than the prospect of meeting this famous illustrator. The boys in the band who overheard our conversation seemed to be nearly as pleased as I. The frisky trap drummer gave a long roll on his drums and a loud crash on his cymbals!

"Ladeez an' gennelmen," he announced, "it gives me great pleasure to make the following announcement: the trumpet player for the El Graucho gets a big break with a big-time artist!"

The fellows in the band laughed and the waiters wondered what he was talking about. The fiddle player leaned over and slapped me on the back.

"No kiddin'," he confided, "I sure hope you get a chance to make pictures for them big magazines. Not that you're such a slouch on the bugle, but who wants to knock himself out in a slap-happy dive like this the rest of his life? Get in a racket where you can have a bevy of

120

them beautiful models floatin' around in your studio all day! *Wow!* That's for me, brother!"

I tried to joke, but playing at night left me little time for drawing. The illustrator might give me a lead on how to go about landing some magazine work which would get me out of this night-life trap. There must be a way to beat the band business!

Around ten o'clock the crowds began pouring into the El Graucho. I was sky-high on my own special mixture of spirits. The manager had promised to jack up the pay for this night, so the boys put extra vitality into their playing.

With midnight nearing, there was still no sign of the famous illustrator. I tried to catch the manager's eye. Finally, in the midst of the melee he looked over and motioned reassuringly that his friend hadn't arrived yet but surely would.

At midnight the place went wild. Couples were dancing around in ludicrous paper hats and blowing madly on tin horns while we were musically blasting in the New Year. The revelers were jammed in, leaving not even an extra inch of room under the tables. Then I saw the manager trying to make his way through the crowd, bolstering up a man who could hardly stand.

The band was easing down on "Auld Lang Syne" to a well-earned intermission by the time the manager reached us. He attempted an introduction.

"I want you to meet—" was as far as he got when my favorite illustrator lunged forward and grabbed the music stand directly in front of me.

"Listen, damn you," he shouted above the noise, staring menacingly at each of us in turn, "I don't want to meet any of you lousy musicians! You're nothing but a lot of dirty rats! Yes, I said rats!"

The manager tried calming him down but there was no use. He was off again, screaming and waving his arms.

"You're all a bunch of lowbrow, marked-down, half-wit rats!"

Fortunately our piano player had the presence of mind to call out, "Come on, fellas, let's give with 'Auld Lang Syne' again! One! two!"

We played it even louder than before, but the music lost itself in the hysteria and the sour and cynical notes from the end of my horn went unnoticed.

121

20

COLLECTOR'S ITEM

*T*HE GARBAGE collector's regular early-morning ashcan cacophony was oddly absent one morning. Ordinarily his crashing, metallic music, which could be heard for blocks around, served as a neighborhood alarm clock. More bleary-eyed than usual, I awoke and squinted out the window wondering what time it was.

It was snowing! Or *were* those snowflakes against the windowpane? Several times before I had been fooled by what appeared to be soft white flakes, but when they stuck to the pane and didn't melt I realized they were only feathers from the pillow factory down the block. So far the winter months had offered nothing but bitter weather, icy winds, and cold gray rains. For some reason I anticipated seeing the city under a deep blanket of snow, maybe because a snowstorm would simplify everything and make the city easier to draw. But this morning it looked just like another feather storm—a false alarm.

Still not knowing the time and since I was now awake, I decided to clean the room and take the accumulation of discarded sketches and other trash to the refuse can outside on the sidewalk. Opening the front door, a spectacular surprise greeted me. The street was being decorated gently by the real thing—not feathers, snow!

While I stood admiring the Christmas-cardlike scene and watching the snow gradually cover the dull and dingy house fronts, the Sanitation Department truck moved quietly up the street with its two collectors, who resembled animated snowmen as they tossed the trash cans back and forth. No wonder everybody was still asleep! The morning's blanket of snow had soft-pedaled their performance.

122

As the truck pulled up in front of my building, one of the men called out, "Hey there, mister! Hallo, hallo!"

At first I couldn't tell to which member of the Sanitation Department the voice belonged. Then the good-natured character on top of the snow-covered rubbish shouted again as he took off his visored cap.

"You no rememba me? You maka pitch my bambino lasta summer!"

It was the uncle of the Italian boy on Mulberry Street I'd met the night of the festival! I asked him about his family.

"Hokay. Everyting hokay. How's by you?"

"Fine and dandy!" I said, actually feeling finer than dandy to think he remembered me.

After he emptied the can belonging to my building and the truck started moving on down the street again, he went right on talking. "I hanga your pitch hup on d' wall of our hapartment. Looksa just lika my bambino!"

All aglow, I watched him pick up a piece of paper out of my morning's trash and look at it. I could hardly believe my eyes. I saw him neatly fold it and put it in his pocket just in time to catch another can of rubbish which his acrobatic partner tossed up to him.

"Why for you trow away lotsa good pitch?" he called back. "I taka this one home give my wife, hokay?"

Of course I waved my consent. The warmth that charged through me at that moment could have melted all the snow on my street if I hadn't run back inside, up the stairs, and begun drawing for all I was worth.

As usual I ate breakfast at the Greenwich Settlement House on Barrow Street near by. This settlement, a godsend for me and for the neighborhood in general, had long been famous for its record of social work under the leadership of Mary Simkhovitch. Through her efforts it functioned as the heart of the village. Families in distress found assistance there, children were cared for, kept off the streets and given free constructive recreation in their after-school hours.

These activities attracted a great variety of people, all concerned with bettering the living conditions of the neighborhood. I was drawn there because of the very friendly social workers themselves and in time several solid friendships were formed. Often Amelia Earhart was there. Whenever she was not flying off to Chicago or Europe she stayed at

Greenwich House with her mother. She was always as interested in hearing about the comparatively mild adventures of other people as in sharing her own experiences in the air.

On this morning of my first New York snow I sat next to her at breakfast, a privilege I took advantage of as often as possible. I couldn't keep from telling her about my happy experience that morning and how it reinforced my decision to start studying at the Art Students' League that very day, whereupon Miss Earhart invited me to drive uptown with her. She also was going as far as 57th Street.

Whisking up Fifth Avenue that morning with Miss Earhart in her sleek, underslung silver roadster was an unforgettable experience. Ear-muffed and red-faced traffic cops signaled her the right of way as she acknowledged their cordiality. It seemed that at any moment the car would take off from the snow-packed avenue and rise above the city into the clouds. In such style Miss Earhart let me out in front of the art school with an invitation to join her again the following morning! To be enrolling in the life class of John Sloan was excitement enough for one day, but this was the sort of thing I had to get used to. New York was becoming a grabbag of surprises.

At the registrar's desk a motherly-looking woman greeted me most cordially, making me feel somewhat like a prodigal son who had strayed away from Art. She wondered why it had taken me so long to get there. It seems that she had received a lot of correspondence from me while I was in San Diego and she brought out my letters from her file. As I proudly dished out my hard-earned orchestra cash for the two months' tuition, she mentioned the fact that it would have been possible to arrange a school loan. Students who found themselves temporarily strapped could take up to five months' study and pay the tuition back later, as long as a year later, she explained.

I felt a little silly when I realized that I might have been studying art on these terms all this time. I tried consoling myself by the thought that if I had been at school how would I have been able to wander around seeing the wonders of the city or experiencing the blunders of Broadway?

The delectable smell of turpentine and the general diligent atmosphere of the famous institution sent me up the five flights of stairs full of saved-up eagerness, even though I went weighted down by enough

125

art materials to redecorate the entire Grand Canyon. From the instant I stepped into John Sloan's painting class, his forceful flow of wisdom made being there seem the rarest privilege anyone could ever have.

The very appearance of the man sang out his greatness: his sharp eyes, jutting chin, his brushed-forward sheaf of steel-gray hair helped keynote his character. Even his brilliant emerald-green tie exposed the fact that his ancestors were Irish. But what he had to say let us know even more convincingly that he came from high-voltage stock. Never in my life had I seen or heard anything to beat him. His words were like sparks and his ideas charged me with a live current of inspiration. Interspersed among his serious remarks was a sharp, deep, and devastating wit.

His criticisms were given in an impersonal manner, never addressed directly to the student whose work he happened to be commenting upon but spoken so that all could hear. Art instruction to him, apparently, was no private affair, it was as public as breathing, and he used our individual efforts merely as a springboard for discoursing on more vital matters. Philosophically, whatever Mr. Sloan had to say on art tied up directly with everything else in the world from nature to politicians. I gathered readily that he was just as vehemently opposed to seeing a student slave away meticulously copying the shadows on a figure as he was opposed to seeing the citizens of the nation complacently putting up with corruption; and he flayed both approaches with his blowtorch honesty. According to him, shadows were merely the absence of light, and if as students we were there to study how to create substance with color, then shadows hardly mattered. Form came first.

His forthright observations of the work upon which he based his remarks made me quite nervous. I dreaded his seeing what I had awkwardly commenced painting. But that first day he was unable to get around to all his students. By the end of the afternoon I felt more at ease, because what he found in other students' canvases that pleased him most was work which, although clumsy, gave evidence of striving. Anything that reeked of the slick made him sick, and he said so in no uncertain terms.

My work certainly came under the heading of clumsiness, but something of the slick also crept in—a mistaken notion of trying to give the impression of competence. All this had to go and a personal expression put in its place.

126

Mr. Sloan encouraged us to feel as free as possible in interpreting the figure as long as we were not influenced by the "photographic." The "camera eye" he called anything that looked flat. "The camera can't think!" he said. "It only photographs lies. If you would believe the camera's statements about nature, you would have to believe that the hand that is nearest you is always larger than the hand farther back. But this isn't so, both hands are the same size—that is, they were before the camera was invented. The artists in the past were never bothered by this sort of distortion—look at Rembrandt, Leech, Van Gogh—they actually resisted perspective!"

Mr. Sloan stayed long after his allotted time that day. Even the hefty model, having put on her clothes, stopped to listen with the rest of us. I thought that perhaps this was a unique session, but every Tuesday and Friday afternoon throughout the following months his generosity of spirit kept the class fastened to his invigorating words while the studio grew gradually dark and his striking silhouette stood out against the skylight.

Something happened to me. Everywhere I went after that I saw color problems, and the city suddenly took on the aspect of one huge canvas; and whenever I saw something especially beautiful I could almost smell oil paint and turpentine. When that occurred I knew I was in love, artistically speaking. Yes, I fell for each section of the city separately and collectively, personally and objectively.

Mr. Sloan made a practice of not allowing himself to get too personally involved in his students' lives. This had advantages; he was not disinterested in each person as a person, he just thought he could give more as a teacher that way. Several weeks had gone by without his registering an opinion about my work, yet he said such pertinent things to me that I realized he understood what I was trying to do. One day, for instance, he commented about drawing crowds. I had a few compositions of that sort to show him. He said the best way to learn to picture a crowd was to learn how to draw the figure. "If you can draw a figure, you can draw a crowd," he told us and he wasn't being facetious. He explained what he meant in detail, so that everyone in the room could hear. "A crowd has a head and a body, not many separate heads and bodies. A crowd is a living, organic mass and as such in making a picture it should be made to work as one figure."

I remember the first time we ever had a real conversation together. I happened to see him in the subway one day on his way to class, so I went up and spoke to him. He didn't recognize me immediately. I had to tell him I'd been a student in his class for many weeks and how much being there meant to me. After that meeting he invited me to one of his superlative parties held in his huge studio overlooking Washington Square. There I had the privilege of seeing many of his great paintings close up and meeting his vivacious little wife, Dolly. There, too, I could observe Mr. Sloan in his gayest spirits. Several of his older as well as his more recent students showed up at these affairs and we saw our serious teacher cutting capers and giving brilliant impersonations. The high spot of these was his pantomime of a distraught banker who gets all wound up in ticker tape while reading the news of his fast-disappearing stock, all acted out with increasing momentum to the music of Ravel's *Bolero*.

128

Studying art the week following this hilarious occasion required something of an adjustment when Mr. Sloan walked sternly into the classroom for his usual Tuesday and Friday criticisms; but it wasn't long before his penetrating, incisive comments turned our attention to the artistic problem at hand. Those days with him meant more to me than I can say. The spin of Fortune's wheel stops only once on such a number and I am deeply grateful to have known and studied with him.

21

STONE AGE

THE SMOKE-FILLED cafeteria at the League rated more adherents to varying schools of thought than any other department of the institution and fiercely enthusiastic discussions were always going on. All the students, however, agreed on one subject wholeheartedly—the importance of food.

Early one noontime while sitting in the lunchroom finishing a bowl of soup, I felt vibrations from several powerful voices emanating from the classroom adjoining. Not a single booming word penetrated the wall distinctly, but rarely had I felt such compelling ardor, especially over art and, if I knew my vibrations, these were certainly most sincere.

Printed on the door of the classroom was *Subjects: Etching and Lithography*. Lithography is a medium for drawing on stone with a greased pencil and it had always interested me, but since I hadn't yet learned how to draw on paper I judiciously put off getting involved with this fascinating process. Now the sounds from inside the class made me think I was missing something.

When the door of the room finally opened a number of industrious and besmudged students came out and went over to the lunch counter,

129

ordered sandwiches and coffee and then sat down at a long table next to mine. Evidently their class never let up because they continued right on talking and making drawings on the white enameled tabletop. The subject of their conversation concerned the way certain of the artists in the past had managed to convey the suggestion of space in their compositions by using figures as projecting volumes.

The most vociferous spokesman of the group, who I guessed must have been a printer since he wore an ink stained apron, started to describe a specific painting by Rubens. Holding a coffee cup high in one hand and a cigarette in the other, he moved his truck-driver's body gracefully into action as he indicated how the old Master had painted angels floating dramatically through space.

It was impossible for anyone to keep from overhearing his remarks. "Just take a look sometime at how Rubens created third dimension by painting those darling dumplings flitting around every which way," he said bombastically. "Hell, those cherubs could be football players the way he has them charging through the composition!"

The effectiveness of the demonstration was immediate. How a person of his build could delineate in gestures the forms of these angels was more than I could understand, yet I saw them and, what is more important, got the artistic point permanently fixed in my mind. Suddenly when the incongruity of his angelic pose struck the lunchtime lecturer himself, he laughed uproariously with the whole cafeteria joining in.

Next day I signed up for instruction in this class and not long afterwards I too was shouting explosively. I found that the lithographic medium fitted my temperament to a T-square. The sensitive surface of the flat stone was so rewarding that it set me to work translating into prints all the random sketches I had gathered about town.

Now my weekly calendar read something like this: Lithographing in the morning, painting in the afternoon and Broadwaying at night.

Weekends it was still Club El Graucho.

22

BACKSTAGE STRUCK

THE SENSATION of coming upon Columbus Circle one winter evening after a day at art school was like stepping into the middle of a symphony. Patterns of people hastening home stood out on the stark whiteness of the snow like black eighth notes on a sheet of music. Avenues flowed from all directions into the center, like the spokes of a great wheel, and there in the hub of the Circle, with the snow skirling around him, Columbus perched high on his podium as if conducting this contrapuntal symphony of taxis, buses, streetcars, and humanity. The glaring General Motors sign flashed on and off, silhouetting the serene, resolute statue. Colossal neon advertisements in every degree of electrical brilliance tinted the falling snow with all the colors of the rainbow. Beneath the surface, the pavements vibrated as the subways kettledrummed their way uptown and down.

A lone chestnut vendor held his place stanchly against the swirling snow and the steam whistle from his little wagon contributed its one note to the night's music. He and I and Columbus were the only ones standing our ground.

It seemed appropriate to have Columbus there looking over the proceedings. By this time he should be wearing an awe-struck stare at the results of his discovery, if the glare from the General Motors sign hadn't already blinded him. Before taking the subway downtown I hurried to finish a sketch of this centrifugal fury, my fingers frozen to my pencil.

Someday, I thought to myself, I'd like to live right here on the Circle and keep Columbus company, for I figured we were practically in the same business—discovering America.

131

The Great White Way must have had a magnet up its long bright sleeve, for no matter what section of the city I felt drawn to, this street of wholesale illusions remained the most irresistible. The greatest cast of characters ever assembled continued streaming along the sidewalks the same as on the first night I beheld its pageant.

Hours were now spent watching and listening to the people who seemed to own the street—the ticket scalpers, the flower salesmen, the organ grinders, the chewing-gum vendors, and the army of solicitors who put in time at their self-appointed posts. I too gradually became one of them, a Broadway beachcomber.

Whenever I didn't have the money for a balcony seat I took to combing the legitimate theater lobbies looking for lost ticket stubs. Between the nickel-swallowing Automat and the various grabby landlords, I was kept nearly drained of spending money. I remember trying one night to fool the management of a successful drama by doing a bit of acting myself. I pretended to be an ardent theater lover waiting for an inconsiderate friend who had apparently given me the brush-off. I began by fretfully pacing the lobby immediately after the curtain had gone up. The lobby was a perfect place to stage my pantomime. I stared earnestly and hungrily at the stills of the stars on the wall and after that I scanned the floor in dismal search for a ticket stub someone might have accidentally dropped. This last charade brought the manager out of the box office. Whether he was touched to the quick or merely wanted to rid the lobby of loafers I could not tell, but he ushered me inside to a comfortable seat in the back row.

Although such Thespian tactics were reserved for only the rarest occasions, I did succeed somehow in seeing almost every play during that season. Like a barnacle, I had attached myself to the theater. When my father back in California heard I was getting in to see the Broadway productions he promptly sent me his prized pair of opera glasses. With them I was able to sit at the back of the balcony and still enjoy such plays as *Cyrano* and *Uncle Vanya*. The glasses put me in the front row.

On nights when I failed to get into a free show, I consoled myself by watching the audience as it arrived for a performance.

133

The audience arrives for an opening night

I also went around to stage doors and watched. Seeing the frail and fabulous chorus girls running to make their cues was a new kind of treat. This stage-door dallying developed into a habit. The sign above one of the stage entrances read: "Through these portals pass the most beautiful girls in the world." When W. C. Fields, who was the star of a current show, passed through those same portals, everybody standing around got a kick out of the incongruity as the great comedian tipped his straw hat and swayed in.

To see backstage life firsthand became an ambition, but I was unable to devise a method for getting past the stage-door man. It took a popular popsicle seller on one of the side streets to introduce me to this glamorous side of show life.

One night I started making a sketch of him. Thinking I was a reporter, he came over and began relating the story of his life. He was interesting but I had to disillusion him by admitting that I was just drawing for my own amusement.

"Sketch artist, eh?" he said. "Well, why not make a picture of me and sell it to one of the papers? You ought to catch me around intermission time in Shubert Alley."

Exposing my ignorance, I asked where that was.

"You ain't never been in Shubert Alley? It's only a couple of blocks from here. I'll have to take you along with me. That's where I get my biggest sales at intermission time. You know why? Well, I'll tell you—there's two shows what have their stage doors opening right into the alley and the casts come tearing out at intermission for a breather and buy me out. You want to come along?"

While we moved down the street together he scrutinized me.

"Never hoid of Shubert Alley, eh? You must be from outa town. Well, I'll show you something to write home about."

By the time we reached the narrow alleyway behind the Astor Hotel, the two shows had begun their break for intermission. The casts came out of their stage doors, exactly as the popsicle man had predicted. The cast of actors in sixteenth-century costumes mixed with chorus girls from a bizarre and breezy twentieth-century musical comedy.

"Whaddid I tell ya?" he shouted over to me while surrounded by his admirers. "Ain't this a panic?"

136

It was not only a panic, it was a picture, and I started making notes. His popsicle sticks worked like wands, for in the next second we were both inside a stage door, where I followed him downstairs directly into the chorus girls' dressing room. The half-clad dancers hardly seemed to mind my intrusion; they didn't even appear to know I was there staring bug-eyed at their charms, they were interested only in my friend and his popsicles. Some of the girls had already made their costume changes for the second act, the first scene of which evidently took place in Alaska as the dancers were fully furred.

When a gruff stage manager found the two of us, we dashed out into the alley again. Fired with enthusiasm I thanked my nervy guide for his tip, and rushed back to my room downtown and immediately set to work sketching a composition—intermission time in Shubert Alley. I knew that the Sunday drama section of the *Herald Tribune* often used drawings of theater subjects, portraits and caricatures of actors and impressions of the current plays. The following Monday morning I summoned up enough nerve to take the finished drawing to the drama editor, Arthur Folwell.

Intermission time in Shubert Alley

The editor was not an easy man to see. There was already a waiting room full of artists anxious to have their stuff in print. One by one they went in and had their moment with the editor, reporting, as they came back with long faces, the same story. In substance, the drama department chief had said that they could leave their work if they wanted to do so but he couldn't promise to use any of it; space in the paper was scarce and, furthermore, he wasn't running an art magazine!

In spite of these discouraging reports, I waited. After another hour my turn finally came up. The drama editor (who looked more like Mr. Pickwick than the monster I had imagined him to be) began his stock speech before he even looked at my drawing.

"In ten years I can't possibly use all the pictures you artists are bringing in here. You better not leave your work on my desk unless you want to lose it," he said, picking up my offering and looking at it quizzically for a moment.

"What show is this from?" he asked.

"From two shows," I answered, thinking he would be pleased at the economical idea.

"Well, you can leave it here on this pile of drawings if you want to, but I can't promise to use it."

"I haven't any use for it myself," I said, feeling suddenly depressed. "I think I will just leave it, if you don't mind."

During the next week I completely forgot about the drawing of Shubert Alley. The cash from a dance-band job enabled me to see a rather fragile play called *Broken Dishes* on the following Saturday night. I was thrilled by the young actress playing the lead. She was wonderful; besides, she reminded me of the girl in San Diego whose photograph was in my wilted wallet.

I remember running around to the stage door unhesitatingly after the play in order to get a close-up of the actress. The stubborn doorman made me wait outside, but when she finally came out I told her how much I liked her acting and she thanked me sincerely. She was even easier to talk to than I had hoped, and all the while continued to recall the girl in my wallet. As we said good night she signed her name, Bette Davis, in my sketchbook.

To celebrate I rushed up the block to the nearest greasy spoon on Eighth Avenue and had a bowl of chili. It was here that one of the biggest events in my life occurred. Next to me sat a man reading the early edition of the Sunday paper. Being an inveterate over-the-shoulder reader, I was enjoying his paper with him when my eyes lit on something that made me gasp. As sure as I was sitting at the counter choking on a bowl of chili, there was my drawing of "Intermission in Shubert Alley" printed, with no doubt about it, on the front page of the drama section of the New York *Herald Tribune!*

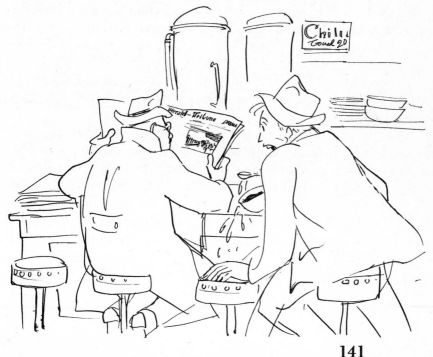

Had the drama editor known what a weekly pest I was to become after that, he probably would have reconsidered before using this first drawing. Every Monday afternoon at four, for the next several years, I appeared at his desk loaded with material gathered from my adventures through the stage doors of all the current productions. Having ecstatically crashed into the theater with this one drawing, it was almost unbelievable to me that such a privilege could also be a way of earning a living—seeing the plays and being paid for it at the same time!

However, not *all* the drawings I showered on the drama department were used, far from it. Two long months went by before another drawing of mine appeared. It seems other artists had to live also. I became used to the routine of wildly opening the Sunday paper to find my drawing had been left out. The editor possessed a special gift for encouraging artists. He did it with such verbose versatility that it was almost worth going to see him every Monday just to hear how he would paraphrase his eloquent rejection.

These drawings as they appeared were paid for by the column; in other words, if a drawing stretched across three columns I would be paid thirty dollars, ten a column. No matter how deep the drawing, it was the width that counted, a fact which may account somewhat for the tendency of my compositions to take on a rather wide rectangular shape!

The appearance in print of this first drawing established necessary proof for the press agents of the various shows that I had legitimate business backstage.

After having once passed through the stage door, I was a goner, given over completely to the fantastic backstage world of scene shifters, electricians, seamstresses, chorus girls, and stars. Now only one problem remained unsolved—the stage-door men! Obtaining an assignment from the paper was difficult, but getting past the stage-door men was murder. These creatures seemed to be mankind's most stubborn inventions since the landlord. Each night it would be necessary to convince one of them that I had authentic business backstage, that I wasn't just coming in to extract some chorus girl's telephone number.

Assuring those keepers of the keys that they could trust me took time and patience but, once their suspicions were calmed, I found them to be the gentlest, most homespun creatures imaginable. In fact, not very long after I was calling them "Pop" the same as everyone else in show business!

Keeper of the keys at the Music Box

"Dad" Collins, stage doorman

Casting call

Choosing the chorus

23

THE STORM MACHINE

IT WAS A BIG DAY when the drama editor actually gave me a full-fledged assignment for the newspaper.

"Try to get me something unusual on this new hit show," he said. "It's a mystery play and there might be some novel angle backstage for you to draw. Anyway, see what you can find."

The curtain had already been up a few minutes by the time I arrived backstage that night. The stage manager greeted me, having been told by the show's press agent to expect an artist from the newspaper. Except for a slight glow from a prop window the entire backstage was in darkness.

The manager, a mere silhouette of a man, shook my hand as he whispered, "I'm sorry it's so blame dark in here. Right offhand I don't know what there is for you to make a drawing of."

What happened backstage in a mystery play was a mystery to me, I told him, but since this was my first assignment I *had* to find something that would make a picture.

"Well, let me see," the manager said, scratching his head trying to be helpful, "there's a storm scene that comes up in the last act—maybe if you watch how our storm machine works, you might get some sort of picture out of that."

This suggestion sounded full of possibilities.

"The storm doesn't come up until around ten-thirty. That's after the intermission. I'll let you know ahead of time. Why don't you sit down and make yourself at home?"

"Fine," I said. "I need a rest." Actually I had never felt so alive and wide awake.

146

"You'll have to excuse me while I take care of an important cue that's coming up in a minute." As he said this he disappeared into the darkness.

I felt around in the dark for the nearest seat but there was no seat to be felt. Edging over to the side of the stage I thought of watching the play from the wings, but the set, being completely enclosed, had no side wings, only a small slit in the canvas backdrop large enough to peek through. With one eye I watched the play and became absorbed in the mysterious proceedings.

No sooner had I lost myself in the plot than a terrifying pistol shot went off behind me. This was probably the cue the stage manager had mentioned. It came, but much too close for comfort. Obviously, someone onstage had just been murdered. There was a commotion at the stage window a few feet away. The window opened and a body was thrown out. The body was an actor and he landed on a thick mattress below. In a good-natured way he immediately came to life, got up, and walked off to his dressing room, through for the night.

Now I was as concerned as anyone in the audience as to who had done it but I was tired of standing. I again groped for something to sit on. In the darkness I thought I saw a barrel-shaped object substantial enough for my weight, and as gently as possible I straddled it.

But a strange thing happened. The barrel slowly began turning under me and before I knew it, I rolled off onto the floor on the other side. It continued to whirl around and around and a deafening racket, like the roar of a tidal wave, came from its insides. As the momentum of the barrel increased, the noise increased. Beyond any doubt, it was the storm machine!

Trying desperately to stop its relentless spinning, I reached out to grab the barrel but grabbed instead a sheet of metal which was hanging from a rope. The metal sheet went wild! It crackled and gave off a sharp, terrifying thunder effect. Even nature in all her anger could never produce more ominous sounds. Bewildered stage hands began cursing in loud stage whispers.

During this disturbance I crept away and hid behind a prop. There I shook, and waited for the storm to subside. I had ruined the play—that was a cinch! As the sounds diminished to the mildness of an April shower I dashed through a side exit.

147

Outside in the theater alley the moonlight shone through the fire escapes. I leaned against the solid brick wall and let the moon soothe my nerves, swearing that I would never go backstage again. Never!

I knew I should be heading for the nearest subway but my feet failed to move. Somehow I couldn't leave the theater. Curiosity had me in a stranglehold. I *had* to know who was the murderer in the mystery play. I must see the final act from out front!

At intermission time the audience poured out to smoke and talk in the fresh night air. The thing for me to do was mingle with the crowd

148

and then walk casually into the theater when the bell rang announcing the curtain. This idea was once given me by a penniless but ardent theater lover who made a habit of seeing the last two acts of all the shows in town.

It worked. When the ushers called "Curtain going up" the crowd began moving inside, stamping out their cigarettes and tossing aside their orangeade cups. I moved in with them. The theater lights dimmed as the rich velvet curtain slowly ascended. There was silence, evidence that the play had held everyone in proper suspense in spite of the premature storm in the first act.

A few people stood with me in the Standing Room Only section in the rear. Everybody in the theater was tense. As the scene opened, the criminal in the play was expected to return to the scene of his crime and the police were waiting for him. I leaned forward in suspense against the back railing.

All at once a woman in the audience let go a hair-curling shriek.

"My God!" she screamed. "Somebody's stabbed me!"

Everyone turned around to see what had happened. Even the actors onstage dropped their lines and stared blankly into the audience.

The shriek had come from directly in front of me. It took me several seconds to realize what had caused the trouble. The woman who screamed wore a low-cut evening gown and she had reason to get excited. During intermission someone had carelessly left a half-finished cup of ice-cold orangeade on the wide railing where I was leaning. I had accidentally pushed it over and spilled its icy contents down her bare back!

I slunk away toward the side exit. The elegant and exasperated woman continued her hysterical fussing while her two escorts called for the ushers to find the fiend. The stunned actors went on with the play, doing what they could to pick up their parts again.

Remembering my assignment for the Sunday paper, I returned backstage.

The stage manager greeted me. "Say, I was wondering where you were," he said. "I didn't want you to miss the storm scene. It will be coming up any minute now. Where have you been?"

"Oh, I just went down the block for a drink," I answered.

Bravely but cautiously, with sketchbook and pencil poised in my nervous hand, I followed him to the spot of my former crime, the storm machine. There in the dim light the enthusiastic stage manager explained the workings of the now-meek contraption.

"So you see," he finished by saying, "inside this metallic basin are thousands of pebbles which when spun around give out a convincing storm effect."

I did my best to appear fascinated. Stage hands were standing around awaiting the cue to send the barrel whirling and to rattle the large, suspended metal thunder sheet.

One of the stage hands, spotting my notebook and undoubtedly presuming I was a reporter, whispered in my ear, "This sure has been one hell of a night. Some idiot actor started the storm machine going in the first act and just a few minutes ago a dame out in the audience lets go with a terrific yelp. She musta fainted or something. Can't say as I blame her—this play sure gives a guy the creeps!"

150

24

THE MILLION-DOLLAR WURLITZER

*F*OR A SECOND assignment I had a somewhat more elevating experience. I was asked to make a drawing of the new stage show at the Roxy Theater. I anticipated this with the greatest interest, having never been inside the mammoth movie palace before.

The publicity agent was on hand to meet me at the stage entrance. This was a break for him as well, he said, because the stage show had never hit the drama page of the *Tribune* and the Roxy had been identified only with the movie section of the paper. He was very obliging and insisted I see the show from the best vantage point, which he thought would be a seat in the orchestra pit. That was as close as I could get without becoming a part of the production.

First he led me understage through long labyrinths of corridors where the musicians and dancers were preparing to take their places. I was introduced to the orchestra leader, Fred Waring, who, having his own ideas about where I should sit, suggested that the best spot would be on the organ seat, since the instrument was not in use during this particular show. Here, he explained, I wouldn't be noticed and yet could have a clear view of the entire production.

The giant million-dollar Wurlitzer rested lifeless at one end of the orchestra pit. After being assisted onto the seat and assuring them that I would be quite comfortable, I took out my sketch pad and pencil and waited for the stage show to begin. The movie was still on the screen. I looked around at the dark audience and beheld the largest mass of concentrated and devoted humanity I had ever seen.

The publicity agent, observing how overawed I seemed, startled me further by reeling off his vast fund of information concerning the fabulous cost of the Roxy enterprise. Being unable to grasp any figure above the musicians' wage scale, I failed to react to his stupendous figures. I was, however, impressed by the fact that I was enthroned on the only Million Dollar Rising Wurlitzer Organ in New York City!

The mushy movie ended with the familiar clinch-kiss fade-out which looked pretty silly from the pit. The musicians began taking their places and tuning up. Precisely at this moment the publicity agent must have leaned carelessly against some button or other, for I felt the organ under me slowly rising. In consternation I looked down over the side and saw the agent staring back at me with a frozen face.

"Hey, stop this thing!" I called over to him.

But it was too late. The organ by now was completely off on its own, ascending into space! As the Million Dollar Rising Wurlitzer rose, the massive mumbling of the audience subsided. Burning with embarrassment I frantically searched for a button labeled DOWN while the organ continued moving up and up. Just as I thought we would go through the ceiling, the organ stopped. I was now suspended in mid-air and, to say the least, the center of attention.

152

Feeling as foolish as I must have looked, I turned around to the millions of eyes bulging out of their sockets. I tried to explain "It's all an accident!" but no one heard a word.

The applause was tumultuous. A piercing spotlight finally found me and helped locate the stopper marked RELEASE and I slowly descended.

Thus ended my first and only appearance at the Roxy. I was never offered a return engagement, although the press agent and Fred Waring and his entire orchestra were splitting their tuxedos as I landed back in the pit.

25

CURTAIN TIME

*A*FTER SEVERAL of my drawings had appeared in the newspapers, including the now defunct New York *World* and the going concern called the New York *Times,* the desire to see something of mine printed on the glossy pages of a magazine prompted me to gather up enough courage to see the editor of Theatre Magazine. The art editor must have had a heart of gold, for right off she sent me out on an assignment to cover a rehearsal of Ziegfeld's *Show Girl.*

Without even taking time to put on a clean shirt I rushed up to the Ziegfeld Theater and presented my note of introduction and, surprisingly enough, there was no argument with the doorman. This was the first rehearsal I had ever attended and I walked unabashed onto the stage where George Gershwin was thumping out the rhythm on the piano for an intricate dance routine based on his latest composition, "An American in Paris."

Dozens of dancing girls were whirling around while others sprawled in a variety of beautiful positions along the benches, resting

153

and reading the tabloids. Three madcap comedians were going through their paces over at one side of the stage.

I was much too nervous and excited to get anything more than a shaky caricature of George Gershwin down on paper. During a break in the rehearsal I met him and he was all I had ever anticipated of my favorite composer.

"You will probably want to get Clayton, Jackson, and Durante in your drawing also," he suggested, and promptly took me over and introduced us. This was Jimmy Durante's first show on Broadway. I remember the first thing he said to me in his attempt to be helpful.

"Do you want me to pose wid me hat or widout me hat? Wid me nose or widout me nose?" he laughed, stamping the floor with both feet at the same time.

Next he looked at the size of my small sketch pad and exclaimed, "Impossible! Impossible! You can get me entire poisonality on that little piece of paper. You shoulda brung along a stone mountain and your carving set!"

Then he sat down for a few serious minutes and I tried another drawing of this dynamic Cyrano. His eyes told all; besides being a great comic, he was a wonderful human being. When I had finished he wanted to see what I had done with his classic profile.

"Colossal!" He jumped up and down and threw his hat into the orchestra pit where he had already thrown at least fifty other hats. "It's insultin'! It's dynamical! I'll sign it!"

Immediately after the rehearsal that afternoon I dove into the nearest subway station and made for my room in the Village, all the while swearing to myself, "If I can't get that girl to come to New York now, I'll give up!"

I wrote a letter trying to describe what had first taken place—my meeting with Gershwin and everything. "How can you resist coming now?" I said. "I'll *not* take 'no' for an answer! I'll not take 'no'!"

Weeks later I took "No, not yet" for an answer, which was probably just as well since my financial status remained as fragile as the city was fantastic.

I had the opportunity of meeting most of the famous Broadway actors and actresses. At first meeting the stars in their dressing rooms made me nervous, but later I found that they were nothing but people with a coating of greasepaint. Most of them put up with my snooping, probably because their publicity agents told them it might mean getting their faces in the Sunday paper.

I also had the privilege of getting to know the unglamorous heroes and heroines of the theater who work the unsung wonders behind the scenes: the seamstresses, the wardrobe ladies, the magic-making electricians, and the curtain runners. Even the highly paid but bored rope pullers who played poker high above the stage on what is called the fly rail used to welcome me whenever I climbed to their precarious perch. They allowed me to make drawings of their activities while waiting for cues which, when given, meant either hoisting or lowering the huge hanging backdrops, transforming the scenes far below. Although these men probably had no idea, and seemed to care less, what the plays were all about, they never missed a cue as long as I knew them.

Once I figured that for one scene between two people a hundred-odd persons were needed offstage. Assisting these two to make love required at least four electricians, a thirty-piece orchestra in the pit, a staff of twenty stage hands, a galaxy of seamstresses and maids, property men and rope pullers, not to mention the all-important publicity men, the box-office managers, and the ushers. Each in his unpretentious way was essential to the production's success.

Celestial activities backstage at "I Married an Angel"

Up on the Fly Rail

A fast game of ping pong during intermission

Maurice Evans
transforms into Falstaff

Walter Hampden
as Cyrano

Lillian Gish in "Uncle Vanya"

Ed Wynn
makes a quick change
in his dressing room

Recess frolic under the stage of "Green Pastures

Hula girls hurry to make their cue

*Scenic designer Boris Aronson
gathers material for a circus set
as the Christiani family rehearses*

Dressing Room only

Supreme Court Justices in a rush backstage at "Of Thee I Sing"

26

SHOOTING STAR

*B*ACKSTAGE at most Shakespearian productions there was likely to be considerable cape throwing and swordplay. You took your life in your hands when you wandered around in the dark behind the scenes. Actors have a way of swinging their flowing garments and weapons with gusto and abandon the minute they are involved in anything Shakespearian.

I remember the evening I almost caught cold watching a certain young Thespian who did more than his share of gesturing backstage before he went on for his performance. This was during the production of Katharine Cornell's *Romeo and Juliet* and the unknown actor who distracted my attention that night was playing the part of a fiery Tybalt. He had only a few entrances to make, but he spent a great deal of time strutting vigorously back and forth off to one side of the wings warming up. He seemed fascinated by his role as he threw his robes around in front of the bored and somewhat bewildered stage hands.

When this actor's sharp eyes caught sight of my sketching, he sensed that I was gleaning subject matter for the Sunday paper. Actors are very perceptive along those lines.

Endeavoring to assist me in my search for material, he took a noble stance directly in front of me and my sketch pad. A shaft of light streaked dramatically across his face as he held the pose for several minutes, undoubtedly believing that he was an irresistible subject. I had other ideas.

I wandered off into the darkness looking for more casual and less obtrusive objects. On the opposite side of the stage I spotted a fireman taking a rest in the wings, where the heavy curtains would muffle his

172

snoring if he happened to doze off. No sooner had I started sketching him than the flamboyant character from whom I had tried to escape came swerving past, slashing the air with his sword and lunging forward onstage.

The fireman was as startled as I, so we both went to a position behind the front proscenium curtain to have a look at this young upstart's performance. Something happened. His performance in the dueling scene was played with such electric energy that you could actually hear the silence of the entranced listening audience. The fireman's mouth dropped open, and he was all ears.

Back in my room that evening I had no choice but to set about drawing this thunderbolt. I looked up his name in the program for my caption. It read: Tybalt . . . *Orson Welles.*

After that it was a pleasure to watch him shoot up like a Roman candle into the Broadway firmament. His Federal Theater production of *Faustus* and the brilliant Mercury Players' productions treated New York to dramatic fireworks. He kindly gave me access to the rehearsals of those shows and asked me to come to one of his first radio broadcasts. From where I sat that night, safe behind a glass-enclosed booth, it seemed merely a good joke, though it turned out to be the performance in which he scared half the nation out of its skin with the Martian invasion.

The theater would indeed be in a doleful lethargy without such dynamic hotfoots as Orson Welles provided to shake it out of its unimaginative rut.

174

27

ELECTION DAY

*M*R. LEBRUN never failed to appear on Mondays for the laundry. Whenever I started apologizing for not having paid the bill, he would always say indignantly, "Did I ask? Let me see what you have painted this week."

Monday after Monday he remained my severest critic. His visits continued to be events of anticipated importance. Whenever I had painted something I thought Mr. Lebrun might like, I would anxiously show it to him, then endure the long moment of suspense. He had a way of looking at the composition, then at me, and then devastatingly asking if my laundry was ready, leaving me limp and depressed for the rest of the week.

There were also Mondays when I tried hiding everything; on those occasions the talk turned to politics and that was a good thing. Mr. Lebrun considered me pretty ignorant about life in the city and also about life in general. He claimed that the theater kept me from seeing the real drama of life outside. My being enthusiastic about everything when there was so much crookedness going on all around annoyed him. Claiming I overlooked the ugly side, the graft and Tammany's rotten politics, he attempted to enlighten me by describing his own experience with grafters.

He told me about the night two young men entered his shop and suggested that he join their "club" if he knew what was good for him.

"What is this club I should join?" Mr. Lebrun had asked them.

"Don't worry, it's a political club—it's a good club and being a member will bring you lots of work."

Mr. Lebrun told me that at first he was a sucker and gave them the five dollars. But nothing happened. His business went along just as badly as before and after a while he began questioning the proposition.

"A month or so later these same men came back late one night," Mr. Lebrun continued his story. "They say for me to pay up the monthly dues to the club. I still ask, what club? What do I get from this club? They don't say anything—just tell me to fork over the five bucks. I refuse."

Then Mr. Lebrun said he put on his cap, turned out the light, went to the door and said to the men, "Here, take the keys to my shop—all the keys. You can have the whole business, I don't want it!"

The men were dumfounded. They didn't take the keys. Instead they stared at him a minute and then left the shop and never came back. But other small shopowners, Mr. Lebrun told me, had been forced to pay protection at the point of a gun and many were given a "ride" without a return trip.

"Well, why can't all the shopowners get together and get rid of these grafters?" I asked him naively.

"Get rid of them?" he answered. "Impossible! You can't get rid of them. They're worse than bedbugs!"

"But how about election time? Can't the people vote their bosses out at the next election?"

"That would be a miracle," Mr. Lebrun exclaimed as he reached for my laundry, "and I don't happen to believe in miracles!"

As election day for mayor drew near, incited by Mr. Lebrun's insinuations about my political acumen. I diligently began reading about local politics. Everyone in town knew it was going to be a hard-fought election. Tammany had its tiger's teeth sharpened and set for the kill. The city government had been held in Tammany's clutches for such a long time that there was considerable doubt if the victims of civic corruption would ever rouse themselves sufficiently to shake loose.

The board of elections in my district met in a tidy tailor shop. The place was thoroughly policed and representatives from the various political organizations were present to prevent any trickery. After casting my vote I decided to spend the rest of the day down on the lower

177

Getting in the vote

East Side, where some of the most hotly contested districts in the city were located.

I have reason to remember a certain barbershop in which the district polling place was located. It was on Clinton Street near the Williamsburg Bridge, for there is where I literally had the closest shave of my life.

Unlike most polling places, where business is suspended for election day, this barbershop stayed open. On one side of the shop three barbers continued cutting hair and shaving customers, while the board of elections took command of the other side. A policeman watched the proceedings.

Small-time politicians, gangsters, and Tammany ward heelers with their crews of hard-boiled henchmen hung around both inside and outside the shop.

When I arrived they watched to see what I was going to do. Their steady glowering told me that they were there for business—which was none of mine. Their business was to guard the polls and see that everyone coming in voted the straight Tammany ticket with no interference or slip-up.

Looking through the window from the outside of the barbershop I tried to observe how the voting was being carried on. Some of the constituents, confused by never having been inside a voting booth before, were assisted by one man who even went so far as to pull the voting lever for them. All this under the eye of the law, which just winked.

The henchmen standing guard outside didn't like my seeing these things. First they tried to run me off by menacing stares. To keep from looking more conspicuous, I decided to go inside and have a haircut.

This turned out to be a good idea. From the barber chair I could watch the continuous line of voters being escorted in by the district boss. He was too busy to notice me but I saw in the mirror that he was surreptitiously passing a dollar bill to every voter as he went inside the booth.

Meanwhile the barber was clipping my hair as if it were grass and his clipper a lawnmower. Half my head was raw before I remembered to tell him to give me only a slight trim. Actually I didn't need a haircut at all.

180

"You come for a haircut—I *give* you a haircut!" the barber said fiercely.

There was nothing else to do but let him continue; besides I was convinced that even a clean-shaven head was a small price to pay for all this staggering information. Watching intently in the mirror I observed one of the political henchmen motion to the barber, call him aside, and whisper to him. Something was up.

When the barber came back to my chair he started ruthlessly cutting my hair again, but now he took a firm grip on the back of my neck. Some barbers have a habit of doing this to keep the head steady, but I wasn't at all sure what this man's intentions were. When he did let go, I realized how tightly he had been holding me and I had to twist my neck around several times to ease the strain.

Just as I started to get up, the belligerent barber again gripped the back of my neck. Then I saw in the mirror that he held a long razor in his other hand.

"Hold still, mister," he said in a garlic-loaded whisper. "If you no hold still—you get hurt! This razor is plenty sharp!"

Sharp razor or dull, I leaped out of the chair, untied the apron from around my neck, threw down fifty cents on the cash register and fled. In a cold sweat I ran to a dark doorway down the street. Having given myself the assignment of covering the election, I was determined to stick around this voting district and see the whole affair through to the end.

Feeling more inconspicuous in the doorway, I made a quick sketch from time to time in my notebook. The people of the neighborhood, who for the most part were poor, decrepit and ignorant, were being gathered up one by one and taken in to cast their votes at a dollar a head. The perplexed and exasperated gangsters kept walking by, trying to catch a fast look at what I was doing. By this time it had become so dark that I could hardly tell what I was drawing myself. Excitement ran high. The street lights came on.

Soaring flames from huge bonfires in the middle of the streets, a traditional part of city elections, towered toward the roofs of the tenements and the kids ran along the sidewalks shouting and waving fiery torches which had been improvised from the political posters.

181

Then a strange change of mood came over everything. Apparently word had come from headquarters that things weren't going as well as they were supposed to for Tammany. Like wildfire the word spread along to all the small-time ward heelers. They forgot me for a few minutes as they scattered around the district putting on extra pressure rounding up final votes. From all directions they returned, each guiding a potential Tammany ballot.

Two of the tougher politicians with turned-up collars all but covering their scarred faces discussed how matters were going.

"Whaddya think is the matter with the vote?" I overheard one ask the other.

"The trouble is the people is gettin' educated. They're wisin' up on us, that's all," the other answered.

While I strained to hear all they were saying on the subject, a short, stubby gangster walked slowly toward me as three others suddenly came up from the rear.

"All right, bud, what goes? What's the racket?"

182

"I'm just minding my own business," I said.

"Yeah? What's yer business? What's that book you got in yer pocket?"

There was no reason not to come clean, so I took out the sketchbook and flipped through a few pages in front of their flabbergasted faces.

"Cripes! He's an artist!" one of the mugs exclaimed. "What in hell are you doin' hangin' around here?"

"Just sketching," I answered blankly.

"Who for?" one of the brighter boys asked. "For what paper?"

"I'm not with any paper. I'm on my own." They couldn't tell how much I wished I *was* working for some paper.

"Where d'yuh live at?" asked the first gangster, who was getting fed up with their small-fry catch.

I didn't *have* to answer any of their questions. I could have remained silent and have been quietly slugged in the doorway. "I live up in Greenwich Village."

With this they gave each other a quick glance. Then one of them said, "Come on, fellas, he's just a crackpot from Greenwich Village. They're nuttin' but a bunch of crazy artists that live up there!"

Another henchman put in his verdict. "Yeah, he's harmless."

I kind of resented this last crack but at least it broke up the meeting.

I had had enough of snooping. Filled with information and still filled with a certain amount of suspense over the outcome of the election, I went uptown to cover Times Square, where the results from the five boroughs were flashed in electric lights on the sides of the Times Building. Thousands of people were already there, a more than adequate assemblage for my purpose, packing every inch of the Broadway area. Everyone was in a fever of expectancy.

By midnight enough votes had been counted for the election to be conceded. The butchers and the bakers, the laundrymen and millions of others—all had pulled a certain lever which made the city theirs. I'll never forget the mighty shout that rose up from Times Square. The city had a new mayor!

His name was Fiorello La Guardia.

183

Election Night, Times Square

My laundryman was right. The theater with its rousing romances and frothy comedies had beguilingly kept me from seeing the real dramas being enacted every day on the streets of the city. Too long the Great White Way had dazzled me by its brilliance.

Now, more than anything, I wanted to continue the pursuit of finding out what made the town tick.

The "project" that the Easter-egg-dye salesman gave me the day of my arrival still held. Actually I had never discovered to my satisfaction where everybody was going and why most of them looked so sad and worried. With me life was exciting and interesting, a condition that made it somewhat difficult to understand why this wasn't the same for others.

Casually across the year I wandered around the various sections of town filling one sketchbook after another, putting down the light and not-so-light fantastic goings-on in summertime, wintertime, uptown, downtown, inside, outside, East Side, West Side, on the sidewalks of New York.

28

HIS HONOR, THE MAYOR

SOME MONTHS later an out-of-breath character appeared at my door and announced that he had been sent by Mayor La Guardia to find me. Imagine that!

"The mayor just wants to see you, that's all," he said.

It seemed that a cartoon of mine which depicted and satirized a day in the life of His Honor had found its way down to City Hall. There could have been only one person who did this mischief—my garbage collector! I remembered distinctly having thrown the copy of this cartoon into the ashcan one morning, and undoubtedly my friend from Mulberry Street had found it and sent it in to the mayor.

186

My breathless messenger told me the sketch had come in the mayor's mail, all wrinkled and without any name.

I greatly admired La Guardia and his untiring concern for making the city gain a conscience, but his numerous activities were irresistible targets for cartoonists and I too tried my hand at it. The only thing that worried me was whether or not the mayor might be angry with my rendering; maybe he thought I was making fun of his perspicacity and perspiration. However, the City Hall scout bounced with joy around my studio while assuring me that the mayor had got a kick out of my effort and that I was to go to City Hall the next morning and meet him.

"Thisa might be the beginning of a bigga new career for you," he said, with a trace of ravioli in his lingo. "Listen to me, I tell La Guardia you need a job. You're starving, see? You have to have a job!"

I told him I didn't see his rambling logic at all. Even if my studio looked a mess and all down at the heels I was certainly not starving, not that week.

"Leave it to me," he fired away. "I pusha you, you pusha me. Okay? You like spaghetti? My wife she make the besta spaghetti you ever eat. You come over to our house Saturday night we have a bigga blowout! It's a date!"

I had no chance to answer his bombastic invitation one way or the other.

"You'll be a bigga shot after tomorrow, maybe you'll paint his walls, make bigga pitch, lotsa money! Me? I do small errands for His Honor so maybe this be a bigga break for me too, who can tell?"

Then standing quite still and looking at me significantly in the eye, he said, "His Honor says to me, 'Mike, I want you go find who makes this here pitch even if it take you a whole month.' So I looks and looks and finally I runs into some fellow by the name of Shellhase a artist and he tells me he think you the one who does it, and so look, I find you in justa four days! How do you like that?"

The Northwest Mounted had nothing on him, I told him, as I nearly pushed him out the door. Naturally, before shaking hands I promised to be at City Hall the next morning at nine.

After a sleepless night of anticipation, I arrived about eight-thirty the next morning, to find the mayor's car already parked in front. Mike

188

met me on the steps, loaded with last-minute instructions. "I hope you know what you going to tell him. Surenhell he'll ask you what kind of job you want, so tell him."

It was still an impossible task to stem his enthusiasm. Logic was out of place, so I said okay. He understood that.

"I found you," he reminded me again. "Remember—I hunt all over town East Side West Side—and listen, that there Greenwich Village is sure the toughest place to find anybody in the world, you know that? I already told the mayor you coming and you need a job very bad, okay?" Mike grew explicit as he led me into the main entrance and passed us through the gate inside. He leaned forward and whispered in my ear, "This is how it's done—I pusha you, you pusha me!"

The waiting room outside the mayor's office was already filled with smoke and heated discussion groups. Mothers with complaints, clergymen and meat packers from the slaughterhouses all stood their turn at visiting the mayor. The packers, large men who would have looked better in butcher aprons, were there trying to settle a meat strike by beefing about the labor situation.

189

Enormous portraits of ex-mayors and other political dignitaries of the past in cutaways and stiff collars hung from the austere white walls. The meat packers who stood beneath these paintings made a curious sight and also made the morning's wait tolerable. I was getting more and more uneasy by the minute. For one thing, I hated to take up any of the mayor's precious time and, for another, I felt all weak and wobbly over what he might be going to say to me. But on top of this I was excited beyond words thinking I would be meeting a man who was truly the people's choice.

My turn came at ten o'clock and a secretary led me into the great room beyond, where I could hardly find the mayor. He was sitting behind a huge desk piled high with important papers and correspondence.

His Honor peered over his glasses and invited me to sit down. Very quickly and succinctly he acknowledged the cartoon I had made, which was on his desk. Between a hundred interruptions a minute he let me know he liked it and wondered if he could get copies made for his friends. I said I would take care of it. Then he asked what he could do for me in return. I knew exactly what I wanted. I asked if he would allow me to make a serious drawing of him at work and he graciously consented. "Right now if you like, only I'm apt to leap out of my seat and sail out over town any second."

During the next few minutes I saw how the heart of the city worked. He dealt with a deluge of problems with the gentleness of a mountain lion; he knew when to be firm and when to wisecrack and never a minute was wasted. A desperate call from the tenants in some uptown tenement came to his attention—no heat. Immediately he had one of his assistants look into the matter and told him to report back in an hour. "They must have heat, do you hear? Some of these land-lords should have to stoke coal themselves!" Then he grew concerned over the price of children's clothing and the rising cost of food. He dictated an appeal. He signed a batch of letters.

His face flashed in a million moods and I could hardly get a sketch finished—each expression was better than the next. He swiveled around in his chair, jumped up, shouted, plumped down again, leaned back, looked up at the ceiling, blew smoke from his cigar with the chugging profusion of a tugboat, buried his head in his hands and thought deeply

190

for a moment before lighting up again and laughing uproariously at something. He was not exactly what you could call a co-operative model. I just had to hold my pencil and watch this human volcano erupt. His movements were as precise, complicated, and graceful as those of an Oriental dancer and it was a fascinating performance. But I knew he wasn't doing it to amuse his spectators; he was bubbling over with energy, interest, and the driving will to get things done. I felt as if I were in the engine room of the city and he was the dynamo.

191

And then, just as he had warned me, an alarm came from the fire department; a blaze had started in Brooklyn and he was off in a streak. He was a blur as he dashed out the door.

My friend Mike had been waiting outside in the hallway the whole while.

"Well, what do you say, ain't he a great guy? Why you take so long? Did he give you bigga job? I bet you didn't ask!"

I told him I was so excited that I forgot all about pushing him.

"Oh, thatsa okay, I was only joking. You taka me serious!"

I took him seriously enough to take him to lunch, where I let him know how much his interest was appreciated. But he never really understood why I wanted nothing more than the privilege of making a drawing for myself of the greatest mayor New York ever had.

29

AN ASSIGNMENT AT SARDI'S

THE DEPTH of despair and hopelessness that was felt by nearly everyone during the depression invaded even the illustrious theater world. I could no longer lose myself in the illusions of plays and musical comedies. I found that among the manufacturers of make-believe the problem of survival was every bit as real and crucial as elsewhere. Hunger and the weight of empty pockets were the common denominator of all working people.

Artists had it bad, I thought, but I discovered that actors had it even worse. For those in the acting profession not only needed to eat, they also had to be seen looking as if they had been eating. Keeping up a good front was at all times essential in their trade.

As a rule the drugstores on the corners served as fairly adequate show windows for these actors who had to let the producers and directors around Broadway know that they were alive and kicking about not having any work. But the best oasis on the West Side was Sardi's restaurant, situated near the shifting sands of Shubert Alley.

Here at Sardi's most of the show folk, whether they could afford it or not, gathered, jabbered, and ate lunch. The restaurant had the reputation of being the birthplace of many a smash hit. Functioning as an innocent bystander along the byways of the theater, I naturally wanted to cover this place where shows were said to be cooked up between antipasto and dessert.

As soon as I had saved enough extra cash, I decided to have lunch there, and while sitting off in a corner of the large room I was able to watch the entire scene without anyone's noticing my sketching. Actually everybody was much too busy eating and talking to see me.

Actors, actresses, agents, producers, composers, directors, and scenic designers streamed in. Newspaper columnists showed up; they found this restaurant a good source of morning copy. The waiters had scarcely enough space in which to swing their trays. Handshaking, cigar smoke and salutations, backslapping and backbiting filled the room. The air churned with productivity.

Near the entranceway Renee was dutifully and beautifully checking hats. Her reddish-blonde hair set the color key for the entire room. It was a room steeped in theatrical history. The walls were covered with caricatures by Gard of the famous people in the profession, many of whom were there in person.

I remember being considerably impressed at being able to listen to Tallulah Bankhead only a few tables away—all she lacked were footlights. I also got a kick out of seeing the newly hailed actress, Katharine Hepburn, whose performance I'd liked in *The Warrior's Husband*. She seemed amazingly unwarlike and serene as she made her entrance into the room. Francesca Bruning, who made such a hit in *One Sunday Afternoon*, walked in with her friend, Mildred Natwick, whose talent for portraying character parts was fast being recognized. Miss Natwick's youthfulness came as a complete surprise to me. I had just seen her convincingly play the part of an elderly grandmother in *The Distaff Side*. In the midst of all this commotion sat Vincent Sardi as overseer, keeping things running smoothly and graciously greeting everyone who entered. Not one of the famous actors who appeared that noon could possibly have held a spotlight more winningly than he.

193

Wet West 44th Street

I returned to Sardi's as often as possible, and late one night, while the last remnants of the after-theater crowd lingered on, I found Mr. Sardi sitting alone at a table finishing a dish of ravioli. For dessert I presented him with a lithograph I called "Sardi's at Noon," which I had just completed for *Stage Magazine*. He was appreciative and pleased and asked me to join him. We talked and I learned a good deal about him and how he had come to be in the restaurant business. Vividly he recalled his boyhood in Italy, when he was forced to sit down at long, crowded family tables for dinner. Those were strict and stuffy affairs and he found them boring, so he stayed on his worst behavior until his grandparents sent him out to the kitchen as punishment. But he fooled them. That was where he wanted to be all the time. He liked the people and the atmosphere in the kitchen, and he developed a flair for tasting foods and preparing them.

Much later he worked in the kitchen of a popular London restaurant, with long hours and tiring duties, and he and the other boys scarcely saw any outside life except through the small round kitchen window that opened into the dining room. Here he dreamed of the day when he could go back and forth freely between the kitchen and the dining room. As soon as he could, he came to America and began working toward the realization of his ambition, a restaurant of his own. He started as a busboy, worked up to a waiter, and eventually became a captain. Finally he had saved enough money to open a small place of his own, and now he owned this world-famous, warmhearted theatrical mecca, which he and his gracious wife Eugenia, whom he had met soon after he landed in America, operated in partnership.

I was fascinated by this story and found it hard to switch my attention when he plunged into another subject. "Do you paint?" he asked, offhanded. I admitted I was a painter by day and a black-and-white man by night. "Do you paint in oil?" I told him I did, puzzled by his queries.

"Well, if you paint, why can't you do for me a series of paintings so I can hang them for my room upstairs? That's just what the new dining room needs, some paintings of the theater."

He wasn't bluffing. He meant it. So I took him up on it and that very night shot back to my room to begin work. Mr. Sardi didn't ask for preliminary sketches or descriptions. Whatever I brought in would be okay, he told me, and he would pay me on delivery of each picture.

For two months during that hot summer I worked on one canvas after another, and as soon as the paint was dry enough I took each one uptown. The series, told in four sequences, was the story of a girl's flight to stardom, beginning when she was a tiny thing dancing to organ-grinder music on the sidewalks of the lower East Side, up through the day she landed a part in a musical comedy through the good graces of the angel who backed the show. The concept was neither an extraordinary nor an original one, but it had a solid basis in fact.

I never have got over the way Mr. Sardi accepted these paintings. He never suggested a thing, he never took advantage of his critical prerogative. He just hung them on his walls, and I ate that summer as I had never eaten before.

30

APPLE ANNIE

*I*T IS ONE THING to observe life shielded behind a sketchbook and quite another thing to be personally involved. So far, most of my knowledge of the city had been gained vicariously in this kind of sightseeing busman's holiday, observing on the sidelines and watching the animated crowds and the general hullabaloo of activity everywhere. Then an experience taught me the value of every individual's life, no matter how unpretentious or insignificant on the surface. I had long suspected that each individual was a separate entity, a world, but now I learned how very important a world it was.

Such a person and such a world was Apple Annie.

Apple Annie sold apples even before the depression. She held down her stand under the fire escape outside the Astor Theater on

45th Street just off Broadway. On my way to and from the theaters I had never given her more than a passing glance. She seemed like some character from a play as she sat there on a bench in her thin coat and faded hat, her feet in their worn shoes resting on a few layers of newspaper to keep away the chill of the sidewalks.

On one especially cold day, after having passed her by hundreds of times before along with the rest of the hurrying crowds, I couldn't resist buying one of her shiny red apples.

"No, business isn't so very good these days," she said, in such a way that I suspected she forgave everyone for running past her.

To hear her speak and to look into her eyes was assurance enough that she was not merely filling a niche under a fire escape to help give Broadway its local color. It was imperative that she sell her apples. After this first visit with her I stopped regularly and we soon became good friends.

Her husband Tom had once been a shoe salesman and now sold shoelaces down in the Wall Street section. One evening as he called for his Annie, I had the honor of meeting him. He was of the same meek who shall inherit the earth—that is, if they can hold out long enough. Both he and his wife maintained a serene dignity seemingly untouched by Broadway.

On the brick wall behind Apple Annie's stand were pasted some wind-torn and faded clippings from various New York newspapers. They were news reports describing the biggest day in her life, the time she was feted and fussed over as part of a publicity stunt for the opening of a movie. She had been whisked around in a limousine to the Waldorf-Astoria and given a suite of rooms, taken to a beauty parlor and dressed in a fancy dress, just for a day.

It was a sad affair for her to remember, if the truth were known, but few people knew the facts. Annie was not one to tell her troubles to everybody she met. What made her feel most unhappy was the fact that certain newspapers had reported that she received a large amount of money for her part in the publicity stunt. This made her friends along the stem, those who sold flowers, gum and newspapers, believe she had earned a lot of money.

"All I ever got was twenty-five dollars," Apple Annie confided, "but everybody thinks I'm a wealthy woman now. I was made a fool of for a day, that's what I was."

198

The one friend on the street who knew more than anyone else how badly Annie felt was Sam, the shoeshiner. He kept his box just a short distance down the block. He knew that when Annie was not at her stand for two weeks after the publicity stunt, it was probably because she became ill from the ordeal and not because she was "too stuckup" to sell apples any more.

"But when she came back, nobody paid her no mind no more," Sam said.

Just before matinee time, when I stopped to see Apple Annie on a bitter cold November afternoon, she asked me if I would mind taking her place at the stand while she went across the street to the Astor Drug Store for coffee. I sat down on the small bench and during those next few minutes I found out what real misery was like. The bricks behind me held the cold like a wall of ice and I was nearly frozen by the time Annie returned. When people walked by without buying the bright apples I began to feel their icy unconcern and callous indifference. My only sale was to a chauffeur who parked a limousine outside a theater, and he eyed me with suspicion.

For weeks I had been wanting to make a painting of Apple Annie and now, when I visualized her sitting beside the radiator in my room, my conscience felt somewhat soothed. She seemed happy over the idea and I asked when she could come. She named the following Thursday as the day to pick her up.

The sun came out on that Thursday and everyone welcomed its unexpected break-through. Knowing who would be the happiest person in the world to see the sun, I whistled along with the rest of the crowd down Broadway. But when I came to 45th Street there was not a sign of Apple Annie at her usual place under the fire escape.

Sam, the shoeshiner near by, said no, he hadn't seen her all that day or the day before either. This was certainly strange since she had scarcely ever missed a day. On Saturday I went up again but she was still not there.

When Sam saw me, he came over holding a folded newspaper.

As he handed me the paper he pointed to a small item at the bottom of the back page. It reported that Mr. and Mrs. Tom McCarthy had died in their sleep from gas fumes from a faulty range in their furnished room at 203 Eighth Avenue. The report ended by stating that Mrs. McCarthy was well known along Broadway as Apple Annie.

The once-exuberant song of the city suddenly modulated into a minor key. Through the frivolous exterior of its gay, swarming crowds I began seeing the cruel gray reality that lay everywhere underneath.

But Broadway as usual lit up like a giant birthday cake and no one seemed to care about or notice the absent apple stand under the fire escape on West 45th Street.

31

MOVING MONTHS

THERE CAME a time when the room in the Village grew much too small to hold the accumulating stacks of drawings and paintings. Before finding a satisfactory studio I moved several times, with each new place offering its own special brand of distraction. These, then, were my moving months, first to one place, then to another.

There was the studio on 53rd Street where a bat paid me frequent visits, beating its weird wings against the skylight. The bat itself wasn't so bad—I got used to it. The trouble came with the landlady, Mrs. Carter, who every day would come into my room and chat, dragging her sugary southern drawl along and taking up a lot of time. Upon giving her my notice one day, I suggested she hang out a for-rent sign ROOM AND BAT, a proposal that sent me out in the street looking for a new place one day sooner.

A slight spell of living in MacDougal Alley followed. Here I had to put up with wild parties in the apartment under me, parties given by a young broker from Wall Street. He tried to live the Bohemian life but he went too far one night by murdering his mistress.

201

The circus tent as seen from my window

I moved again. The next place, a large loft over a garage on West 52nd Street, was a rare find. Mr. Rossini, the landlord, was also the manager of the garage. He willingly rented the loft as he had been feeling miserable about the standstill business his garage was doing. For some reason very few automobiles were coming in for repair, a state of affairs which was fine for me since the empty garage below meant no annoying gasoline fumes or backfirings. Yes, this quiet loft promised to be the best place yet.

But the long sought-after sanctity ended abruptly. In New York the last thing anyone expects to happen is sure to happen. A circus came to town and parked itself in the empty lot across the street! The day the elephants arrived I wondered where in the world they would be kept. While I wondered, Mr. Rossini schemed. He cheered up when he got the idea of turning unctuous host to several cages of tigers, three elephants, two jumping chimpanzees, and one goose which he parked in the rumble seat of an old Cadillac. They were all housed in the garage space directly under me!

The new rent-paying tenants were a docile lot the first day and I went to sleep that night without worrying too much about the heavy breathing of my odd bedfellows below. Around three A.M., however, one of the tigers let out a fierce, hair-raising roar and I fell out of bed. In a few minutes the entire menagerie went berserk. The goose in the rumble seat must have got loose somehow and started all the hullabaloo. The elephants began blasting the air with their trombonelike shrieks and the chimpanzees shook their cages in frenzied rage.

This same jungle jamboree occurred every night, and as a consequence I was never able to feel very safe behind my feebly latched door. Mr. Rossini, who only a short time before had been in the dumps, was now blasé and very pleased with his animated prosperity. He heeded not my daily complaints; it seems *he* slept at home in Brooklyn! His only suggestion was for me to try to consider these circus performers as fellow artists! That's when I gave up.

Columbus Circle had never lost its interest as a spot where I hoped someday to find a place to live. Then, after vainly scanning the Circle at least ten times over and with the plan of living there all but abandoned, I caught sight of an old weather-beaten sign dangling over a doorway which definitely stated that there was an apartment for rent three flights up.

204

On the top floor I found a large, forsaken dentist's office, perfect for a working studio and a wonderful place to live, with several windows facing out over the Circle. I immediately unhooked the FOR RENT sign and ran to the real estate office and plunked down the first month's rent before I dared let them know I was an artist. But because of the constant noises from the traffic and the soapbox haranguers below, plus the general pandemonium around the Circle, this apartment had been considered undesirable anyway. To me all this commotion provided endless subject matter. The entire city seemed to propel itself past my windows.

The first major event after settling on the Circle was the installation of a telephone. This, almost more than anything else, gave me the feeling of at last belonging to the metropolis, and even more so when the Manhattan telephone directory was delivered. I felt as elated over seeing my name included in this book as some people must feel about being listed in *Who's Who*.

All those long months I had never forgotten the girl from the art school in San Diego or allowed her to forget me. Letters describing the Circle had been flowing in torrents out to California. Shortly after

Freedom of Speech, Columbus Circle

moving into the studio I could no longer stand the distance between us and, inaugurating the new telephone one night, I called California.

After hearing her say "Hello" on the other end of the wire and my operator say "New York calling," I started playing into the receiver a three-thousand-mile serenade on my battered trumpet—I still remembered how to play "Someone to Watch Over Me." Amazingly enough she was still on the other end when I finished, so I popped the question, and six months later she arrived in New York pretending to be on her way to Europe to study art!

32

PLAYING IN A PLAY

*O*NE OF THE first evenings after settling in the new studio a few friends were sitting around listening to a pal of mine, Eddie Mayehoff, play the piano. He was pumping life and satire into some old melodies, and after a while I chimed in with my trumpet, which had been hanging on the wall serving as a holder for paint brushes. But every so often when I felt like blowing off steam, the brushes would have to go. On this particular evening we were playing all the old-time tunes we could think of when the doorbell rang. The windows were wide open and so we thought that some soapbox orator down in the Circle had come up to complain of our annoying blasts. As it turned out, it wasn't a Circle soapboxer, it was William Saroyan. That's New York for you. Leave your window open, and a playwright appears at your door.

"Heard the music so I thought I'd come up," he said as he took off his dapper hat and came inside and met everybody. "Go ahead, keep playing. It sounds great, especially from four blocks away! Incidentally, what's the name of that tune you finished playing just now?"

"An oldie called 'My Wonderful One,' " Eddie said. And without further coaxing we began playing it over again. The evening went on with more music and then talk. Saroyan didn't stay as late that night as the others because he said he had to get back to his hotel room and finish a play he was writing and hoping soon to direct and produce.

Early the next morning I was surprised to receive a phone call from him. He asked me if I would mind meeting him at the Automat for breakfast. He seemed excited.

Over coffee and scrambled eggs he showed me the newly prepared script for his play. It had taken him all night to finish it. One part which had been of minor importance was now enlarged. Specifically, he explained, the part was for a character named Harold, a long-lost brother, who returns in the final act blowing a horn as he walks up a hill toward his family house. He asked me to read this new material. Then he said:

"You see, the play has to have the brother coming home—and I want *you* to play the part."

I stared at him.

209

"Moreover," he continued casually, "I particularly want you to play that tune, 'My Wonderful One,' offstage during the first two acts."

Although I appreciated his confidence and enthusiasm I told him the notion was absurd, ridiculous, and completely out of the question. He seemed surprised that I reacted this way. He'd thought I'd get a bang out of doing it. For one thing, I told him, I respected his play too much and in addition to not being an actor, the way I played the horn was strictly corn.

"That's why I like it," Saroyan said, again urging me to consider his simple request. "Think it over a day or so. I'll call you later."

Since I promised him I'd think about it, I did, but not too seriously. When I spoke to my caricaturist friend Al Hirschfeld the following day I told him about Saroyan's preposterous proposal. He didn't think it was so crazy.

"So what?" he said. "Aren't you backstage in some theater nearly every night anyhow? Aren't you always blowing your horn? Why not just combine the two and have some fun? Besides, you'll be having some valuable experience on the side, learning how it feels on opening night on the other side of the footlights. It's only a couple of hours out of a long day. What can you lose?"

One needs encouragement to make a fool of oneself.

The next day Saroyan called for his answer. I said all right, but on condition that he chop off a hunk of dialogue at the end. I could never have memorized such a lengthy speech.

"Great!" he shouted over the phone. "I'll knock off all but three lines for you to say."

The next thing I knew I was a member of Actors Equity, in the cast, signed, sealed, and slightly astonished.

Rehearsals began almost immediately. Three people had never had speaking parts before but the rest were experienced troupers. Eugene Loring had been a ballet dancer and Betsy Blair had danced in a musical comedy chorus before Saroyan convinced her that she fitted perfectly the part of the leading girl.

Being in complete charge of his play, the author instituted a novel method of directing. After reading the play through a couple of times he left the actors and actresses alone for a week or so, telling them only to feel out or "find" their parts for themselves. The cast seemed to take

210

this as a tribute to their instinctive insight, though after a few days we began to wonder. Deliberately refraining from interfering too soon with his actors, Saroyan spent most of his time in a tavern across the street where he held lengthy sessions with ex-jockeys, a man who played two clarinets at the same time, and an old man dressed in fur skins, who called himself Daniel Boone and went around town writing God-fearing mottoes in white chalk on the sidewalks.

Finally the day came when the playwright did have things to say and the play began to take shape miraculously. Saroyan made a few slight suggestions at first, and he made those apologetically, not wanting to offend his cast who had indeed "found" and felt their parts fairly well by this time. He gave the performance the timing, accent, and intimacy it needed.

During this period I had a comparatively easy time, with nothing to do but memorize three short lines and blow "My Wonderful One," like a memory or an echo of the past, every time the name Harold was mentioned. Some days the cast rehearsed scenes in which the name was not mentioned at all, and then I drew instead. I even made a poster for the play. It looked for a while as if it was all going to be a snap.

But then the ogre of Opening Night began leering at me from every seat in the empty orchestra and every row in the balcony. I started jumping around in my sleep at night like a kangaroo. Those three lines at the end of the final act lined up in front of me and each word was like a flaming hoop through which I had to leap. It was a nightmare. I might easily stumble and fall into the orchestra pit from the long ramp on which I had to enter. The valves in my horn might get stuck in the middle of a measure. I could easily run out of breath. But the most likely thing of all to happen would be for me to hit a sour note and send the audience into a spasm of laughter.

I phoned Hirschfeld frantically. "You don't know what this means!" I screamed. "My life hangs in the balance on what happens opening night. You don't know what it's like! You just sit back in your barber chair and make caricatures. It's hell, I'm telling you. Living hell!"

All Al would say was, "Take it easy. Take it easy. Think nothing of it. I'll catch you if you fall. I'll be there in the front row!"

On opening day, although the curtain was not scheduled to go up until 8:30, I arrived at the theater around two in the afternoon. The

212

stage was silent, ominously silent, empty and black except for the faint work light off to one side. I must have oiled the valves of my trumpet fifteen times. Then I began going over my lines and walking through my part completely unaware that I was being observed by a stage-door man who had nothing better to do at the time than to stand idly in the wings.

"If I'm not being too personal, what in Sam Hill are you supposed to represent anyhow?" he said, throwing me completely off balance. "This is sure the darnedest play I ever did see."

I tried explaining my part to him before I realized how hammy I had become, defending my characterization just like a full-fledged actor. So I gave up and went out for a light supper.

By 7:30 the members of the cast were all in their respective dressing rooms busily making up. I had to look like someone who'd been on the road for forty days and since I was already a wreck there wasn't much for me to do but to spill some dust over my suit.

The playwright sent each of us a reassuring, richly poetic, fifty-word telegram telling us we were the hope of the theater. Al Hirschfeld thoughtfully sent me a secondhand gas mask from an Army and Navy store.

When the stage manager called "Curtain! Places, please! Places, please! Everybody onstage!" I went promptly to a small anteroom off to one side of the stage and shut the door. The idea of playing my horn in here was thought up by Saroyan, who wanted to give distance to the sound. As the melody was to be heard but faintly during the first two acts and more distinctly in the third, this effect of gradually approaching was to be achieved by opening the door slowly as I advanced forward and onto the stage. A member of the stage hands' union had been assigned to stay in the room and open the door for me. The cue to start playing the memory melody was given by the stage manager. A mere twist of the doorknob was his signal. I really got to know that doorknob well by the end of the evening.

It was difficult to imagine that on the other side of those cold brick walls sat a critical Opening Night audience. For a split second I allowed myself to think back to the days in San Diego when I played this same tune while accompanying a Victrola record by Paul Whiteman. It was one of the first records my father gave me.

213

Waiting for the doorknob to twist wouldn't have seemed half so frightening if the stage hand had been less glum and bored with the show. He thought it would be the biggest fiasco he'd ever been party to. There's a legend in the theater that stage hands have some fine instincts about what does and what does not go, though they refrain from telling the actors what they think. They just look gloomy and say nothing. Their faces reproduce their innermost thoughts, and I saw only too plainly what was written on the face sitting beside me. He was already packing up the sets and loading them onto the truck for Cain's Warehouse. He took to reading the sports page in the evening paper.

Two minutes before my final cue he turned to me and said, "I see where Fats Walkowitz pinned down Zebatzo the Doll, at the Garden last night."

"You don't say?" I managed to squeak as my throat went chalk dry. The doorknob twisted and I started to blow. The stage hand calmly put down his paper and opened the door for me to go out. As I left he whispered in my ear, "Good luck, pal!"

214

Somehow the play came off that night. As far as I know everyone remembered their lines and amazingly enough I didn't fall into the orchestra pit. After waiting up all night with several friends and driving around Central Park till dawn when the morning papers would appear, we rushed to Times Square to find how the play had fared with the critics. We could scarcely believe our eyes as we read the reviews at four A.M. For the most part the critics were heartily in favor of *The Beautiful People*. The play had a few months' run and received one of the Critics' Circle awards that season.

I don't know about the rest of the cast but in spite of our good times I for one could never go through another Opening Nightmare for anything. It was like taking a Turkish bath in a goldfish bowl.

33

ROMERO REVISITED

7HE DAY BEFORE Thanksgiving that year was one of those fine fall days of which only New Yorkers can boast. No falling leaves are needed to tell them that fall is in the air. Something else happens and it acts on the populace somewhat as does catnip on a cat. Countless numbers of people are strapped to their offices and factories and aren't permitted the luxury of wanderlust, but I was one of those footloose free-lancers and the fall weather intoxicated me.

I had just finished making a drawing for the Sunday drama section and was on my way downtown to deliver it. The editor had warned me that the deadline had to be one day earlier than usual because of the midweek holiday. But I forgot about the deadline and the drawing and carelessly I found myself wandering around a part of town I had almost forgotten—Tin-Pan Alley, my old hunting grounds. The streets were full of melodious memories, abetted by the slippery sounds of

215

saxophones and trombones oozing out of the windows of the rehearsal halls. A few years earlier I had paced those pavements with a horn in hand, and now I was doing it with a pencil. The horn had come in mighty useful in those days but a pencil was much more my weight. At least no greasy sidewalk bandbooker could give me the fast dodge. Although I felt no special longing for a return of those days, the familiar haunts threw me into a nostalgic tailspin.

Above the hawking cries of the news vendors and the sad-sour music of street peddlers, the worn, lone voice of an old-time sightseeing bus guide rang out. His chant had not changed a syllable in all those years.

"All right, folks, take a sightseeing trip around New York! See the magic island of Manhattan, Chinatown, Wall Street, the Bowery, East Side, West Side, all around the town—see the wonder city!"

In a cloudburst of recollections, I began thinking of all the people who had helped open the doors of this fabulous Manhattan mansion for me: the popsicle salesman, Al Romero, the stage-door men, the press agents, and a legion of others. I earnestly wished that I could tell each one of them just how much I appreciated what he had done to boost my spirits. This wish could not have seized me at a more propitious moment, for directly in front of me stood the Gaiety Building where Al Romero had held down his show business office. Could it be he still operated there? Wasting no time wondering, I rushed inside and took the jerky elevator to the fifth floor.

It was a thrill to see Al Romero Enterprises still stenciled on the door. It was ajar, as always, and I could hear someone plunking on the piano inside. Then I saw Al sitting there, the same old Romero, busy as usual talking into the pay phone planted on his desk.

After he hung up the receiver I stepped in and eagerly stretched out my hand. "Hi there, Al!" I shouted. "Remember me?"

We shook hands but it was plain that he didn't recognize me. Had I grown so out of shape?

"I'm the guy you used to give all those trumpet jobs to," I said. "Hennington Hall, the Minnehaha Club, the El Graucho, remember?"

"Oh, sure, sure, trumpet man!" he finally tuned in. "Well, how the hell are you?"

216

I said okay, and asked how were things in the band-booking biz.
"Terrible!" he groaned and looked dejected just the way he used to.

"I just came up to tell you how much I appreciate what you did
for me when I first landed in town, dishing out all those jobs. You
probably didn't know it but you darn near saved my life—" The words
weren't sounding as sincere as I meant them, but I stumbled on while
Al got up nervously from his chair and went over to the large window
that overlooked Broadway. He put one foot on the radiator, then
interrupted my speech. Talking to me although he said the words out

the window, he muttered, "Sorry, Mac. There's absolutely nothing happening around here. Not a thing for trumpet. The street is deader than hell."

While he was saying this, the phone rang. He dashed back to answer it. I tried vainly to let him know that I hadn't come up hinting for a job, but it was no use. He looked up from his phone conversation, holding his hand over the receiver, and said, "Listen, pal, give me a ring later, say around New Year's—things may loosen up by that time, eh? I can't do anything for you right now."

I knew the cue: Exit smiling.

Back down on Broadway the sightseeing-bus man was winding up his sidewalk serenade for the day. "See New York," he chanted. "Come, see the wonder city, Chinatown, the Bowery, Wall Street! Bus leaving in ten minutes!"

I felt sorry for those visitors who believed they could know the town by glimpsing the public buildings, the historic landmarks and the parks, when to know New York one had to get next to the living landmarks, the people. The only hitch in this personal conviction was that there were too many inhabitants for one person to get next to. But whether or not it was logical, my insatiable appetite for seeing everybody continued unabated.

On the corner of 48th Street, while waiting for the traffic signal to turn, I suddenly realized that W. C. Handy, the renowned Father of the Blues, had his music publishing office right nearby. Once I had promised myself that someday when I got up enough nerve I would drop in on him. I wanted to shake hands with this man Handy.

Now there was no excuse. New York had given me plenty of gall. I hesitated, but just then the light turned green and said "Go." I immediately headed for his office.

Handy had been important to me when I was a kid playing the horn. The jazzy wail of "St. Louis Blues" sailed into my soul. His music taught me that the blues is a mood not limited to St. Louis or Memphis but is apt to crop up anywhere, anytime, in the streets and in the lonely rooms, night or day.

Luckily for me Mr. Handy was in that afternoon. Not only was he in, he made me feel almost as if he had been expecting me. We were introduced by a faithful secretary as he cordially invited me to have a seat alongside him.

It seemed so wonderful just to be there that I hardly knew what to say, so I came right out with my admiration for the "St. Louis Blues." He really seemed pleased that I had brought up the subject. The minute I mentioned it he called to his assistant who sat pecking out a new melody at the piano in the corner, to bring me an autographed copy from the files of both the "Memphis" and the "St. Louis Blues." Signatures as such had never meant much to me, but this one was different. It was his, full-bodied, artistic, and free.

I began trying to explain how his music always seemed to me to be a kind of musical cement which kept the aching hearts of America patched together, but my metaphor got stuck somewhere along the line, and Mr. Handy let me know he was grateful for these sentiments.

Everywhere I could see framed photographs and letters from almost every musical celebrity worth mentioning. They had all inscribed their names and words of highest esteem. My pipsqueak enthusiasm seemed trivial.

As he sat smiling, looking trim and in full command of his affairs, he made me feel perfectly at ease while I tried sketching in my notebook as if I weren't intruding on what certainly must have been a typically busy day. He said that most of his daytime hours were spent here in his office attending to the business of protecting the rights to his old songs and the publication of new ones.

"And in the evenings I'm always playing my cornet at parties and special functions around town wherever my services are needed. I play the 'St. Louis' straight. Most people have never heard it played that way, the way I originally wrote it."

At this point he stood up, elegantly erect, and put his hands out in front of him as if he were holding his horn to his lips. Then he gave a vocal interpretation of how it should be played. I could hear the brassy, clear-cut notes, and it sounded better than I have ever heard it. When he finished, he said simply, "Like that. Not fancy or orchestrated, just as written." He sat down and then asked, "Where did you say you first heard my Blues?" When I told him California, his face gleamed like a brightly polished coin. "That's where I got my first newspaper notice in Sacramento in 1897. I was leading a minstrel band at the time, and they wrote it up. I still have a copy.

"But to get back to the blues," he said, sensing that this was what I most wanted to hear about. "They used to say the blues belong to the Negroes. They called it Negro music. But I've lived to see the day it is accepted as just all-around American music. I remember once a band leader who led a band in the First World War, telling me that whenever they played the 'St. Louis Blues' to the troops overseas, the boys all shouted for more. They called it 'home' music. 'Give us more of that home music,' they used to say. Those boys didn't know that the reason they probably liked it so much was because they were feeling the same things I felt when I wrote it—about people being separated from their loved one. The blues came out of that—sadness, anger, and lonesomeness."

More phone calls started coming in and there were other distractions, so I felt it was time to leave, but before doing so I let him know what a privilege this short visit had been.

"You make me feel like I was somebody," he said as we shook hands. Imagine the papa of the blues saying a thing like that!

His secretary led me to the door and graciously assured me I was welcome any time. I told her that when my drawing of him was finished I would bring it in and let him have a look at it.

"Mr. Handy would be very happy about that," she said. "However, you understand he is unable to see now. Both his eyes are impaired. I do the seeing for him."

I had not even suspected it from his alert, perceptive demeanor.

34

NICKEY

*U*NTIL THE TIME I met up with a boy named Nickey, children in the city had appeared to be merely grace notes scampering up and down the scales on the scores of sidewalks. Not that they were insignificant or unimportant factors in the theme of things, they were just elusive and difficult to get next to, to really know. I had sketched them many times, swarming in the streets in the sweltering summer heat, enjoying a free dunking from an unplugged water hydrant.

221

The old swimmin' hole . . . .

. . . . *East Side version*

And in the wintertime, too, I had watched them sliding down the snow-covered hills of Central Park, snowballing and shouting. They went with the scene of the city like popcorn with the circus. They could be seen on all the neighboring rooftops flying kites and training pigeons. I saw them dancing for pennies around Broadway late at night, then scurrying off through the crowds and vanishing. On other occasions I had noticed them eager to help their families in their struggle for survival—like gamins they gathered papers and cardboard cartons and wooden boxes for fuel. But always they slipped quickly out of my sight whenever I became most interested in following them up.

Through knowing Nickey the city suddenly took on a new and terrifying dimension.

That Thanksgiving Eve, while I was having dinner in the Automat right off Columbus Circle, two boys and a waif of a girl came running in through the revolving doors looking as if they owned the world. Dodging in and out of the crowd, they raced up and down in front of the food display windows which were like jewel cases to them. At first these avid young vagabonds acted as if they would ransack the place and devour the entire stocks, but when their frantic searchings began to slow down, it became apparent that they were determined to be selective and buy wisely, since they had only a few nickels to spend.

After every item in the Automat had been considered and appraised, the oldest member of the trio, an eleven-year-old he-man from Hell's Kitchen, rounded up his cohorts and gave them some instructions.

First he advised the little moll to be sensible-like and buy herself a glass of milk. Then he ordered his other pal to go over to the dessert section and purchase a piece of chocolate cake. Then he went over to the beverage section, plunked his nickel in the slot, and came back with a cup of hot coffee.

Losing no time they captured a table and prepared to consume the feast. A paper napkin was tucked under each urchin's chin and then the master of ceremonies set about sharing their purchases three ways. With the skill of a trained chemist he divided the milk into three empty glasses and then doled out his coffee into the milk, making three equal portions of café-au-lait with cake. All this was done without the slightest thought of the many eyes fastened on their antics. I could imagine Mrs. Blass here—how she would have stepped in and managed their careless little lives!

Only after a few swallows the bottles of seasoning in the center of the table could not be resisted. With a wild tangle of arms and hands they doused their concoctions with catsup, vinegar and generous sprinklings of salt and pepper. Now the poor gourmands really began eating in earnest.

I sat back in agony waiting for the inevitable eruption, which was not long in coming. The feminine member became the first to meet with reversals.

As her face gradually turned pale green she moaned to her headman, "I think I'm getting a little sick, Nickey!"

That was all she needed to say. Nickey, the leader, leaped to his feet, caught her in his arms and dragged her away from the table.

As he headed past me he asked in a hoarse whisper, "Hey, mister, which way's the ladies' room?"

A half hour or so later when the little girl was feeling herself again, they abandoned the Automat. I saw all three of them outside standing around the subway exit, and when I passed by Nickey recognized me.

228

"Gee, thanks a lot, mister, for helping me and my goil friend," he said, aglow with appreciation.

Then his large eyes spied the drawing pad I held in my hand and before I had time to stop him, his fingers were racing through the pages.

"Hey! You're a artist, ain't you, mister? Look, fellas, this here guy's a artist!" He shot his words out in rapid fire. "That's what I want to be, a artist! I draw too!"

"Yeah, he draws real good," his pals chimed in.

"Today I drawed a picture in school of a lighthouse with the water and the storm and a ship and everything! We was all supposed to draw something to repersent safety. It was Safety Week at school, you see, and the teacher she puts my drawing right up on the wall. Didn't she, Henry?"

Henry backed him up. "Yeah-man, I seen it!"

I couldn't keep Nickey's fingers from filing through the pages of my sketch pad. He caught sight of the drawing I had made of him in the Automat.

"Hey! That's *me*! Holy smokes! He made a picture of me! Hey, mister, can I have it, huh?" There was no holding out on this request. It was his.

229

However, I wanted very much to make another drawing of him for myself. If Nickey would come to my studio just a block away for a few minutes, I might make a serious study of him. I asked if he would mind.

"Sure, why not? We'll all come up!" He swung around to his two pals. "Listen, gang, this here artist is going to make a picture of me and we're all going up to his place. Come on, let's get going!"

In a few minutes they were scrambling up the three flights of stairs ahead of me, looking like a section out of a sideshow, pushing, shoving, and shouting. While fumbling for my keys outside the door, I felt foolishly like a trainer and his troupe. But the desire to make a drawing of Nickey was irresistible.

No sooner had I unlocked the door than the three terrors dashed all over the room. Henry and the little girl discovered the piano and began to make music with their filthy little fingers. Nickey flew almost immediately to the corner window, which overlooked Columbus Circle, and before I knew where he had found them, he was manipulating my prized opera glasses. Holding them to his eyes, he lost himself in his imaginary lighthouse tower overlooking the asphalt sea.

I went about getting some materials ready for the drawing. If only I could catch him the way he is now, looking out the window, I'd really have something, I thought to myself. But it was impossible. Nickey wouldn't hold still a minute. As he leaned farther and farther out the window I became panicky and had to pull him back.

"But I can see me pop!" he shouted.

"Your pop!" I said. "Where?"

"He's way up there in that big building. Yeah, there he is now! I sees him in the window!"

I tried to get Nickey to point him out but it was obvious that no one could be recognized in any of the thousands of windows. My friend had a very vivid imagination.

"What's he doing now?" I asked, attempting to keep one jump ahead.

"Oh, he's a waiter. He's waiting on tables," Nickey answered, slowly lowering the glasses. "Say, mister, can I have these here spy-glasses so I can keep an eye on me old man? Can I? Huh, mister?"

230

As he had taken a possessive grip on the opera glasses, I realized I should be more firm. After I had carefully explained the need for them in my work and told him that they had been given to me by my father years before, he quickly dropped the subject and put aside the glasses.

"Now, let's sit still a second, Nickey," I said. "I want to start the drawing of you."

Nickey, carried away with curiosity, ignored the request and raced wildly about the room from one object to another. Fortunately the duo-piano team was still lost in its music. Finally Nickey came upon some of my paintings, mostly of theater subjects, stacked over in one corner.

He picked up one canvas after another, exclaiming, "Geez, you're a painter, ain't you? I wisht I was a painter too! But I never get a chance to paint nothing!"

"Why not?" I asked, unable to keep from prying into his private life.

"Aw, when do I get any time? I got to cook my own meals and go to school."

"You cook your own meals?"

"Sure. My pop and mom, they both work."

"What does your mother do?"

"Oh, she's a actress."

"Well, is that so!" I said. "I see lots of shows—maybe I know her. What show is she playing in?"

"Well, she ain't exactly acting right now," Nickey admitted, slowly unwinding his fabrication, "but she acted once in a play what the union give over on Tenth Avenue—they give it two nights! She's really a waitress, too." His face saddened as his imagination gave out. "She works at the Taft Hotel and we're going to have turkey in the kitchen tomorrow! A real party after they serve the hotel people!"

Here Nickey paused to look his predicament straight in the face. "My folks don't get much time to be around home. You see, they work most of the time. Besides, they don't care much what I do anyways."

"Well, they *have* to work, you know," I said, "and they're probably trying to fix it so that someday—"

Nickey interrupted me. He had no patience with smooth talk. "Aw, what the hell. My pop's a good guy and he's a member of the union."

He went on looking through the paintings. "Say, mister, where was you borned at?" he asked abruptly.

"California. Why?"

"Geez, that must be some place! I sure wisht I was borned there! I ain't never been out of this here city but once. That was when I went to the country for three days. Geez, I remember there was mountains and trees and horses, and I seen a long, long river! I'd give two hundred billion dollars if I could go live in the country!"

There wasn't any more chance of getting Nickey to sit still than of getting a jack rabbit to pose for a portrait. I gave up trying to make any sort of finished study of him. Finally I said, "Say, you kids ought to be getting home. It's darn near eight o'clock. Besides, I have to get on downtown to do some work."

"Yeah, sure, my pop's home by this time, I guess," Nickey said politely. "We got to scram too. Listen, mister, any time I can help you out or do anything for you like clean up the place or sharpen all your pencils or anything, let me know!"

232

I handed Nickey some change for his trouble and led the trio to the door. At the head of the stairs they all put on their best manners. Then in a torrent of gratitude they flew down the stairs into the night, like little demons.

After cleaning up the studio, which looked like the aftermath of a bargain basement sale, I went downtown to the theater to make drawings of a new musical comedy. There in the dissimilar backstage world of dazzling artifice, I saw nothing but Nickey's face with its intense eyes and piercing expression of desperation. Somehow there existed

between us a deep kinship. He seemed to be the very image of me when I was his age, except our dreams were going in opposite directions. I had wanted to live in the city just as desperately as this boy wanted to live in the country, and we both sought the freedom to find ourselves.

Later that night, when I came home and opened the front door, a strange wind swept through the large room scattering papers all about. A window must have been left open, yet I distinctly remembered having closed all of them. As I looked around, the evidence of dirty hands showed everywhere, familiar very small handprints. I located the one open window and leaned out and saw that a long pipe led past the window to the roof just above.

The intruders must have gone to the roof and shinnied down the pipe to the window, climbed in, investigated the place, and then fled in a hurry. I found nothing missing—not a thing. With this perplexing mystery to confound me further, I went to bed.

Thanksgiving Day has always been an especially colorful event on the Circle. The annual Macy's parade of giant figure-shaped balloons passes the wide expanse on 59th Street and then floats fantastically on down Broadway, almost dwarfing the high buildings. Even Columbus's statue looks like a mere toothpick. My window offered a perfect place from which to view the entire proceedings.

The parade was to start about eleven o'clock, but people began gathering long before. Children, conforming to the unique Thanksgiving Day custom in New York, were masquerading in grownups' clothing, the boys decked out in their mothers' cast-off finery and the girls dressed in remnants from their fathers' closets. These ragamuffins, as well as the plainly dressed children accompanied by their parents, collected early along the sidewalks in eager expectation of the parade.

On previous Thanksgivings I had enjoyed fully the annual spectacle, but it all seemed much different today. I knew that it would take more than the biggest balloons in the world to give the children of the city what they really deserved.

While I was watching out the window, the front doorbell rang and continued to ring impatiently until I opened the door. There, to my astonishment, stood Nickey and his pal Henry, both dressed in Thanksgiving Day finery.

Nickey was wearing a long, full skirt and a large, dilapidated hat decorated with flowers, under which his rouged and powdered face was hardly recognizable. Henry wore a purple dress and for a hat he had on his own red knit stocking cap with a feather stuck in one side.

Nickey was the first to speak. "Happy Thanksgiving, mister! We just come to tell you happy Thanksgiving!"

"Thanks. Same to you," I said, stepping out into the hall and closing the door behind me. The mood had distinctly changed since the night before.

Henry, hiding behind the flowing skirts of his leader, began pushing.

234

"Go on, Nickey, tell him, tell him! You know, like you said you was going to."

Nickey punched his pal for talking out of turn.

"You don't need to tell me anything," I interrupted. "I know all about your breaking in."

Both boys swung around, almost falling off balance, their mouths dropping wide open. "We didn't break in! Honest to God we didn't," Nickey cried.

"Then what *did* you want last night?" I asked, as Nickey fell back against the wall stunned by my uncanny detective work.

Henry pulled down his red knit cap all the way over his embarrassed brown face and sputtered, "Mow me down and bake me in a pie!"

"Yes, I know all about it," I said, "so you might as well tell me what you were after."

At this point they both wanted very much to run, but Nickey was too curious to find out just how I got wise to the "job" they had pulled.

"We didn't do nothing, honest, mister artist!" Nickey reiterated, looking down at the floor.

Henry rolled back the knitted cap from his face. "Go on and tell him, Nickey, like you said you was going to."

"Yes, what is it you want to tell me?" I helped Henry prod.

"Well," Nickey began, "we come to tell you we was going by your building here last night and I hears your telephone ringing and it keeps on ringing and I says to Henry, 'I bet he ain't home and he wants his phone answered,' so we runs upstairs and your door is open—"

"But we rings your bell first!" Henry interrupted.

"Yeah, we rings your bell first, and then we goes on in and I answers the phone."

"Who was it?" I asked.

Silence for a second, and then bewilderment. Then Henry quickly clinched the story. "Nobody. They just hung up!"

Nickey could hold back his curiosity no longer. He blurted out, "Say, mister, where do you hide all your money at? We looked all over the place and we only found three lousy pennies in a milk bottle!"

"Let's get back to how you got into the apartment," I said, vainly trying to keep some logic in the discussion. "You fellows went up to the roof and shinnied down the pipe and came through the bathroom window, didn't you?"

Henry again pulled his cap over his face. "Mow me down and bake me in a pie! I guess he knows everything!"

Nickey slapped the side of his own terrified face. "My golly, mister, what are you going to do to us?"

Following a moment of quiet distress on the part of all three of us, Nickey's face slowly took on the look of an innocent and frustrated child. He started to cry, rough, frightened sobs.

Coming up close and clinging to my arms, he said, "Please, please, mister, don't tell my pop—please don't! They'll send me away to a reform school! My mother wants to get rid of me. She ain't my real mother—she wants to get rid of me and send me away!"

I did my best to find the right words and the right thing to do. Henry sat down on the top step and was patient.

"You won't tell on me, will you, mister?" Nickey pleaded. "I want

236

to go to the country, I always wanted to go the country, but I don't want to go to no reform school even if it is in the country!"

As he was saying this, the faint, tinkling sound of band music from the Circle outside drifted into the hallway. Nickey's eyes popped open wide as wet saucers. He looked at Henry who jumped up, and now they were both looking at each other.

"It's the parade! It's the parade! Holy smokes, the parade's started."

Nickey let go of my arms and gathered up his skirts.

"Hey, mister, let us look out of your big front window, will you, huh?"

I opened the door and in a flash they were inside, running straight to the window screaming with delight.

"Geez, this sure is swell, mister. We can see the whole parade better than anybody in the whole city!"

As they leaned out the window, Nickey turned around for a second, looked me squarely in the eye, and said, "I hope you noticed I didn't take your father's spyglasses last night!"

Out in the Circle band music filled the air, mixing with excited shouts from the crowd. The monstrous rubber figures resembled gargantuan robots as they floated down the street. Each balloon took at least twenty men holding ropes to steady it.

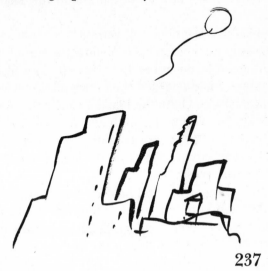

237

Then a child accidentally let go of its tiny five-cent red balloon. As it gently sailed free, up and up over the tops of the buildings, all eyes, completely ignoring the parade, turned to watch its infinitesimal flight.

Nickey, one of the first to spot the small balloon's breakaway, put his arm around his pal Henry and whispered, "Geez, don't you wish you had ahold of the string? I bet we would land somewheres far away—like maybe way out in California!"

35

COME ONE, COME ALL

*I*MMEDIATELY after the parade my two window guests departed, but not before promising that they would visit me only on the condition that I be present at the time. They went their rambunctious way while I went solemnly to Staten Island for Thanksgiving dinner with friends.

The genial conversation and warmheartedness of my hosts, not to mention the turkey dinner, helped mellow the troubled thoughts about Nickey and the sad fix he and all the other city kids like him were in.

By sundown I had boarded the ferry and was heading back across the bay to Manhattan. Off in the blazing sunset the city looked vaguely toylike and simple. The high buildings were but neatly piled blocks; and as I leaned against the forward rail of the boat that late November afternoon, I began having the same feelings as when I first ferried to the island from the West.

The glimmering city ahead held the same magnetic spell over me as on that day, but with one great difference: although the island visually appeared to be serene and simple, I knew how deceitful was this pictorial aspect. After what I had already seen and learned there, I

238

knew that within these steel and cement walls millions of lives were complexly bound together. All had come there by either choice or circumstance, even as I who was one to come quite willingly; and I too found myself inextricably bound.

Why, then, considering all this, did I feel such a tremendous eagerness to reach its port?

The darkness of evening quietly and imperceptibly cloaked the city in magnificence. Despite the fact that I had not intended to allow its surface beauty to claim me, I stood there in reluctant reverence absorbing the spectacle.

Overhead the sea gulls wove a wreath of movement around the boat, dipping and soaring almost as if they were guiding us to our destination. In just those few seconds while watching their flight, the city had taken on a shimmering effulgence; millions of windows were lighting up the buildings and turning the island into an incandescent carnival of chandeliers and Christmas trees. I suddenly had the warm and wonderful feeling of coming home. I knew for the first time in my life what I had been searching for without ever being wholly aware of it—home—and home was now Manhattan.

Being a part of this seething, turbulent, fabulous family was a privilege that brought with it a living proof which no one could ever take from me, proof that all people could live together if they but would.

A light spray of salt water splashed over the side of the boat, gently dousing the passengers with a bracing blessing as the ferry moved into the welcoming arms of the slip.

239

36

SPRING IN THE CITY

*C*AME SPRING and came the girl from California and I could not help being extremely delighted and personally proud of the show my city put on for her welcome. New York emerged from the long winter with all the eagerness of a young bear romping out of hibernation. The population flocked into the sunshine seeking every opportunity to get out from under the cold gray shadows. Central Park flourished with enraptured couples. "Keep off the grass" signs lost all authority—everyone broke the law and nature ruled supreme.

Perhaps I was biased, but spring in the country could be no match for spring in the city! Seasonal signs of the earth's awakening were everywhere. In the windows of the drab tenements mattresses bloomed, pillows popped out on fire escapes with all the profusion of an orchard of blooming apple trees.

Wagons loaded with bright flowers appeared on street corners in every part of town. Even the sad and haggard horses sported decorative nosegays and trotted gaily down the street. Children tried getting closer to the sun by flying their kites off the rooftops.

Yes, the city in all its grimy glory helped me win over my girl Lydia to my way of life. Her name now became synonymous with spring. It was love at first sight between her and the city and soon afterward we were married in a little church around the corner from the Little Church Around the Corner.

Word reached California about our matrimonial amalgamation. Not having heard from my old guardian Mrs. Blass for such a great while, it came more or less as a shock when a letter finally did arrive. She seemed not to be quite her buoyant self, probably because she

240

learned that the girl was of my own choosing and not hers. At any rate, she made a fair attempt at congratulating us, as her letter shows.

My Dear Boy [she wrote], I have heard through your father that you are to be married and I want you to know I am very happy if you are. Naturally I would give a great deal to be there with you both and make toast for your breakfasts but things do not always work out the way we hope, do they? I am especially glad to hear that the girl you have selected is a California girl; that alone makes me feel I can approve of her. I only wish she might have visited me before she went to New York, I should like to have told her some of the things I know about you, not ever to feed you parsnips, etc., or have you learned to like them?

I have been so very busy with my school here. I go from early morning to late at night trying to instill good behavior in my young people. They make it very difficult for me sometimes yet I love them all. Let me tell you a secret: last year I did have a proposal of marriage myself but I could not dare consider it. I am too set in my ways and besides my walnut grove is my main extracurricular interest. Oh, did I tell you that Hortense, you remember her, she

241

sends her love too, well, she is staying with me. Her husband Sylvester got in some trouble at the bank and they had to break up.

Isn't it fine about Warren's doing so well in the hotel business? I hear from Botsford's mother occasionally and she tells me Bots is doing very well with an engineering firm up in Spokane, Washington. I always thought he would turn out mechanically. And lovely Ada Staley, I hear from her father, has just finished a very successful tour around the country with some symphony orchestra. And that is all my news. When summer comes I will welcome a rest as I am really not well and I may go to my sister's in Cassopolis. This letter is mostly about me but it is prompted by the news of you. If there is anything I can do for you, any advice you might ever need, please do not hesitate calling on me, for I am, as always, with love,

Your Auntie Carrie

Our honeymoon was spent revisiting all the places I had written Lydia about. She had to see Mulberry Street, Orchard Street, and the Bowery, and of course Broadway. We took our time wandering around. Sometimes we got caught in sudden spring showers, but nothing stopped us from sketching almost everything we saw. I hadn't dared

242

hope she would feel as I did about the city but there she was, driven to make water colors and drawings of the city with the same elation as I had first felt. She found subjects I had blindly passed by. It seemed incredible to me that I could have skipped so much.

Eventually she met all my friends, who accepted her unanimously as I knew they would. Still, in all the excitement of introductions, I harbored one fear: Mr. Lebrun. My unpredictable laundryman had followed me all over the city as I moved from one room to another. Would he take exception to her? In the event that he did, I would have no choice but to get a new laundryman and that was a mournful prospect. Since he had never approved wholeheartedly of anything that I'd ever painted, how could he approve of someone I had chosen as a wife?

Knowing how honestly concerned he was over my spiritual progress, I subtly mentioned this matter to Lydia, who was quite prepared for the crisis.

I had forgotten about its being Monday on the day Mr. Lebrun came to pick up the wash. He entered the studio puffing from the three long flights of stairs, and I tried to make him comfortable in a chair before presenting him with the surprise announcement.

"Where have you been lately?" he panted. "You're never here when I call."

I waited for him to catch his breath before taking it away from him again. Lydia was in the kitchen and I went in to tell her the moment of the great meeting had arrived, and advised her to bring along a glass of cold water in case Mr. Lebrun choked with shock.

As I ushered her into the studio, Mr. Lebrun had already been busily giving his familiar once-over to several drawings which lay on the table. I prepared Lydia to hear the worst as I made the introduction.

Mr. Lebrun met the situation like a man; more than that, he met it with a Frenchman's gallantry, kissing her hand and then both my cheeks; but nothing could hide his surprise as he surveyed us both quizzically, back and forth, up and down. Then he broke his own stilted silence by telling Lydia how he had been my severest critic for years and how he had been patiently waiting for the day when he could come right out and say in all honesty and with confidence that he had found something of mine which he considered Art.

243

"It so happens—" he continued in his attenuated, suspenseful way—"it so happens that this morning I have seen a picture here which I think is by far the best thing, if not the only thing of his which has—shall I say—Soul, and I believe every real work of art must have that. I want to congratulate you!"

As he spoke he picked up a small water color of an old lady selling gum at the entrance to an El station. Beaming like a man who has just caught a hundred-pound barracuda, he held this drawing up, full of affectionate esteem.

"Now this is what I call Art!" he shouted. "What's more, I want to buy it! How much?"

The picture he held in such merit was Lydia's, painted only the day before down on Rivington Street!

I couldn't have been happier if it had been my own.